P9-DZZ-760

Exploring Canada

THE NORTHWEST TERRITORIES

by Gordon D. Laws and
Lauren M. Laws

LUCENT
BOOKS®

THOMSON

GALE

LIBRARY
FRANKLIN PIERCE COLLEGE
RINDGE, NH 03461

San Diego • Detroit • New York • San Francisco • Cleveland • New Haven, Conn. • Waterville, Maine • London • Munich

© 2003 by Lucent Books. Lucent Books is an imprint of The Gale Group, Inc.,
a division of Thomson Learning, Inc.

Lucent Books® and Thomson Learning™ are trademarks used herein under license.

For more information, contact
Lucent Books
27500 Drake Rd.
Farmington Hills, MI 48331-3535
Or you can visit our Internet site at http://www.gale.com

ALL RIGHTS RESERVED.
No part of this work covered by the copyright hereon may be reproduced or used in any form or by
any means—graphic, electronic, or mechanical, including photocopying, recording, taping, Web dis-
tribution or information storage retrieval systems—without the written permission of the publisher.

LIBRARY OF CONGRESS CATALOGING-IN-PUBLICATION DATA

Laws, Gordon D.
   The Northwest Territories / by Gordon D. Laws and Lauren M. Laws.
      p. cm. -- (Exploring Canada series)
Summary: Examines the history, geography, climate, industries, people,
and culture of Canada's Northwest Territories.
Includes bibliographical references (p.) and index.
  ISBN 1-59018-049-6 (hardback : alk. paper)
  1. Northwest Territories--Juvenile literature. [1. Northwest
Territories. 2. Canada.] I. Laws, Lauren M. II. Title. III. Series.
  F1060.35.L39 2003
  971.9'2--dc21
                                         2002156055

Printed in the United States of America

Contents

Foreword   5

INTRODUCTION   **North of Sixty**   7

CHAPTER 1   **Land of the Northern Lights**   11

CHAPTER 2   **The First Peoples and European Exploration**   25

CHAPTER 3   **Toward the Twentieth Century**   41

CHAPTER 4   **Life in the Territory Today**   55

CHAPTER 5   **Arts and Culture**   69

CHAPTER 6   **A Territory in Transition**   81

Facts About the Northwest Territories   95

Notes   99

Chronology   101

For Further Reading   103

Works Consulted   104

Index   107

Picture Credits   111
About the Authors   112

Titles in the Exploring Canada series include:

Alberta

British Columbia

Manitoba

Ontario

Quebec

Saskatchewan

Yukon Territory

Foreword

Any truly accurate portrait of Canada would have to be painted in sharp contrasts, for this is a long-inhabited but only recently settled land. It is a vast and expansive region peopled by a predominantly urban population. Canada is also a nation of natives and immigrants that, as its Prime Minister Lester Pearson remarked in the late 1960s, has "not yet found a Canadian soul except in time of war." Perhaps it is in these very contrasts that this elusive national identity is waiting to be found.

Canada as an inhabited place is among the oldest in the Western Hemisphere, having accepted prehistoric migrants more than eleven thousand years ago after they crossed a land bridge where the Bering Strait now separates Alaska from Siberia. Canada is also the site of the New World's earliest European settlement, L'Anse aux Meadows on the northern tip of Newfoundland Island. A band of Vikings lived there briefly some five hundred years before Columbus reached the West Indies in 1492.

Yet as a nation Canada is still a relative youngster on the world scene. It gained its independence almost a century after the American Revolution and half a century after the wave of nationalist uprisings in South America. Canada did not include Newfoundland until 1949 and could not amend its own constitution without approval from the British Parliament until 1982. "The Sleeping Giant," as Canada is sometimes known, came within a whisker of losing a province in 1995, when the people of Quebec narrowly voted down an independence referendum. In 1999 Canada carved out a new territory, Nunavut, which has a population equal to that of Key West, Florida, spread over an area the size of Alaska and California combined.

As the second largest country in the world (after Russia), the land itself is also famously diverse. British Columbia's "Pocket Desert" near the town of Osoyoos is the northernmost desert in North America. A few hundred miles away, in Alberta's Banff National Park, one can walk on the Columbia Icefields, the largest nonpolar icecap in the world. In parts of Manitoba and the Yukon, glacially created sand dunes creep slowly across the landscape. Quebec and Ontario have so many lakes in the boundless north that tens of thousands remain unnamed.

One can only marvel at a place where the contrasts range from the profound (the first medical use of insulin) to the mundane (the invention of Trivial Pursuit); the sublime (the poetry of Ontario-born Robertson Davies) to the ridiculous (the comic antics of Ontario-born Jim Carrey); the British (ever-so-quaint Victoria) to the French (Montreal, the world's second-largest French-speaking city); and the environmental (Greenpeace was founded in Vancouver) to the industrial (refuse from nickel mining near Sudbury, Ontario, left a landscape so barren that American astronauts used it to train for their moon walks).

Given these contrasts and conflicts, can this national experiment known as Canada survive? Or to put it another way, what is it that unites as Canadians the elderly Inuit woman selling native crafts in the Yukon; the millionaire businessman-turned-restaurateur recently emigrated from Hong Kong to Vancouver; the mixed-French (Métis) teenager living in a rural settlement in Manitoba; the cosmopolitan French-speaking professor of archaeology in Quebec City; and the raw-boned Nova Scotia fisherman struggling to make a living? These are questions only Canadians can answer, and perhaps will have to face for many decades.

A true portrait of Canada cannot, therefore, be provided by a brief essay, any more than a snapshot captures the entire life of a centenarian. But the Exploring Canada series can offer an illuminating overview of individual provinces and territories. Each book smartly summarizes an area's geography, history, arts and culture, daily life, and contemporary issues. Read individually or as a series, they show that what Canadians undeniably have in common is a shared heritage as people who came, whether in past millennia or last year, to a land with a difficult climate and a challenging geography, yet somehow survived and worked with one another to form a vibrant whole.

North of Sixty

W ith boundaries now north of the sixtieth parallel, the Northwest Territories is an untamed and uncompromising land. The freezing temperatures and brief daylight of the winters, and the vast distances between settlements, make the territory a challenging place for people to live. The landscape and weather can change dramatically and even deceive the unwary with mirages of imaginary mountains across the horizon. At night, the northern lights brighten the winter traveler's evening but disrupt communications and wreak havoc with power grids. Only the most hardy plants and animals make their homes in the great north, yet even their survival can be threatened by minor disruptions to the ecology. But the harshness of the climate and starkness of the landscape are also among the attractions of the territory. The wilderness is virtually pristine—many of the territory's parks have no access roads—and it is the chief tourist attraction for thousands of people.

Before Europeans arrived, the area was occupied for thousands of years by native peoples. Contrary to popular beliefs about the ceaselessly grim life of the frozen north, the land provided many of these native groups ("First Nations") a healthy, even prosperous way of life. The Inuit (formerly known as Eskimo; Inuit is the society's own term for themselves—"the people") who thrived on whale and seal hunting had leisure time sufficient to develop sophisticated arts comparable to many of the Great Plains tribes to the south. Dene (deh-nay) tribal groups in the central and southern portions of today's territory had also lived in parts of the land for thousands of

Canada's Capitals and Major Cities

years. (Formerly known as Chipewyan, Dene, like Inuit, is what these people call themselves.) But the native way of life was altered and disrupted with the coming of Europeans.

Beginning some five centuries ago, the land began to draw explorers searching for the elusive Northwest Passage, a hoped-for sea route across the top of North America that would shorten the trip from Europe to Asia. The Northwest Passage would turn out to be impractical—it was not successfully navigated until the first years of the twentieth century and only a few score times since then—but the push north and westward spawned an intermingling of cultures that continues to this day.

After the explorers came fur traders and prospectors and with them a host of mysteries and legends—gold mines thought to be just over the next mountain, men apparently starved to death or perhaps murdered, settlers driven to madness by the frozen climate. During this time, native peoples and Europeans met and began cooperating, but diseases and exploitation and land conflicts ultimately created the root of many of the tensions that exist to this day between natives and nonnatives.

A New Identity

As it has been since its creation as a distinct jurisdiction in 1876, the Northwest Territories is a political entity in flux. Its identity has changed numerous times over the past 125 years as large chunks of its area have been carved out of it to make other provinces and territories. The most recent of these border changes was in 1999 when Canada created the new territory of Nunavut. This basically cut the Northwest Territories in half. Even so, the Northwest Territories remains a huge area, larger than Texas and California put together. Within its far-flung borders are the two largest lakes entirely within Canada's borders and the second-longest (after the Mississippi) river in North America.

Spread out over this vast domain is a sparse population of thirty-seven thousand people. The territory has long been home to aboriginals who have thrived in the frigid north, and today only Nunavut has a higher population of aboriginal people among the provinces and territories of Canada. With such a mix of people, conflicts and social problems are unavoidable. The resource-driven economy flows hot and cold, services such as education and health care are expensive to deliver, and land disputes can be difficult to resolve.

■ *The Northwest Territories' capital of Yellowknife spreads inland from the shores of Great Slave Lake.*

But the possibilities that drew explorers to the north and kept aboriginal peoples in place offer hope for the future. From the territory's earliest days, its foundation has been its natural resources. Today gold mining is in decline, but new findings suggest that the territory is one of the richest potential sources of gem-quality diamonds in the world. Industry and native corporations are working to build a natural gas pipeline that would benefit Canada and give native peoples huge revenues, guaranteeing them financial stability for years to come. A mix of European descendants and aboriginal peoples now collaborate in government halls and live together in the territory's small population centers. Much needed revenues are beginning to alleviate some of the social ills that have plagued the people of the far north. Ultimately, the Northwest Territories' northern location and fragile ecology, its huge but perhaps impermanent size, its natural-resources-dependent economy, and the distinct nature of its population are the main factors that have driven its history and will determine how the area will adjust to its latest—if not its last—identity.

Land of the Northern Lights

As harsh as the land and climate of the Northwest Territories may seem, the great north offers a varied landscape, including unusual plants and animals and some of nature's most striking oddities, such as the northern lights. Covering more than 450,000 square miles (1.1 million square kilometers) and comprising 12 percent of Canada's land, the Northwest Territories takes in arctic and subarctic extremes. It has a severe climate with freezing temperatures occurring potentially anywhere in the territory during every month of the year. Even so, the somewhat more temperate southernmost strip of the territory is home to a wide variety of plants and animals, and it is misleading to think of the territory's overall landscape as barren.

While freezing temperatures have reigned for millennia, researchers now believe that aboriginals saw the great north as teeming with large game and life-sustaining wildlife. One aboriginal explained, "The land is just like our blood because we live off the animals that feed off the land."[1] In short, the Northwest Territories is a land of striking contrasts, of life surviving in the harshest conditions.

A Frigid Climate

The Northwest Territories has one of the more severe climates of any inhabitable place. Approximately one-third of its land mass is located above the Arctic Circle and is thus exposed year-round to the icy winds that can sweep across the multiyear (permanent) sea ice that exists in much of the Arctic Ocean. (So-called seasonal sea ice forms in the fall around the islands of the southern Arctic archipelago but melts back during the summer.) The Mackenzie Mountains along the territory's western edge also block rain- and snow-holding clouds, making much of the central and eastern portion of the Northwest Territories relatively dry. Norman Wells, in the center of the Mackenzie River valley, for example, receives an Arizona-like seven inches (seventeen centimeters) of rainfall yearly.

Cold is ever-present. Subfreezing temperatures can occur during the summer in even the warmest place in the territory: Fort Smith, on the Alberta border, experienced a low of 26° F (−3° C) in July 1951. The frost-free period is typically limited to a mere forty to sixty days north of the Arctic Circle. In

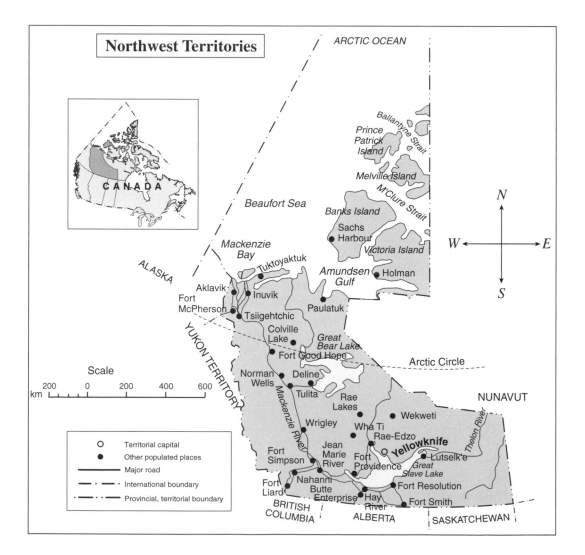

Sachs Harbour, on Banks Island in the Arctic Ocean, average daily highs even during the summer are in the 40s F (5° to 10° C). The average daily low for January in Sachs Harbour is a brutal −27° F (−33° C).

The somewhat more temperate southernmost regions of the territory may enjoy one hundred frost-free days. Summers in Fort Smith, for example, are moderate, with average daily highs in the low 70s F (low 20s C). Winter in the south is still long and cold. In Yellowknife, average daily lows from December to February range from −17° to −21° F (−27° to −29° C).

Much like temperature, precipitation varies in the territory, with the greatest disparities between the arctic and subarctic regions. Though snow covers the ground at least eight months of the year in much of the Arctic, snowfall is not excessive. For example, Sachs Harbour receives an average of only 41 inches (105 centimeters) of snow and 2 inches (5 centimeters) of rain annually. Many locations below the Arctic Circle get more precipitation, with Fort Liard in the far southwest among the rainiest places in the territory. It receives about 12 inches (30 centimeters) of rain annually. Most of the communities below the Arctic Circle get about 4 to 6 feet (120 to 180 centimeters) of snow per year. Even so, blizzards in the north can create whiteout conditions with visibility reduced to a few feet. Hearne describes one such storm that overtook his group on its way to Great Slave Lake:

> A heavy gale of wind from the North West put us in great disorder. The wind blew with such violence that it overset several of the tents, and mine, among the rest, shared the disaster . . . as the tent-poles fell on the quadrant, and though it was in a strong case, several parts were broken, which rendered it entirely useless.[2]

Overall, climate is probably the most critical factor affecting the lifestyles and movements of the territory's residents. The bulk of the territory's population is located in the more southerly regions, yet even there travel can be risky for much of the year. Difficult travel conditions can shut down boats, planes, and automobiles, and an automotive breakdown in a remote area could prove disastrous to unprepared travelers.

A Rocky Foundation

Another key determinant of life in the Northwest Territories is the varied landforms. The majority of territory land sits atop the Canadian Shield, the solid layer of dense rock that

■ Days Without Light and Nights Without Dark

When British explorer Samuel Hearne arrived on the north side of the Great Slave Lake in late December 1771, he complained in his journal that the days were so short "the Sun did not, at its greatest altitude, rise half-way up the trees." In contrast, the daylight during summer is extended, and this longer daylight period actually allows some plant life, which would be hindered by the otherwise short summer, to thrive.

The exaggerated length of nights and days stems from the far northern location of the territory. During winter when the earth's northern hemisphere is tilted away from the sun, sunlight barely reaches the area of the Arctic. The reverse is true during summer—the far north is tilted toward the sun and receives near constant exposure to its rays. The effect grows more dramatic the farther north travelers go. Hay River on Great Slave Lake receives twenty hours per day of sunlight during mid-June, while the Inuvik area experiences almost a full twenty-four hours. With the approach of the winter solstice on December 21, daylight grows shorter. Few places in the territory, however, experience complete darkness for even a whole day. Rather, on the darkest late-fall and early-winter days, most areas experience several hours of twilight without the sun ever rising, with the length of this twilight time being longer in southern areas than in northern areas. In such cases, the sun's light is bending through the atmosphere, providing a hazy light even though the sun never appears above the horizon. Only in the uninhabited Queen Elizabeth Islands of the extreme north are parts of the territory completely dark for days at a time.

■ *Time-lapse photography shows the progression of a Northwest Territories "midnight sun."*

serves as the geologic foundation for much of Canada. This rock layer is covered by little topsoil in most areas and, in general, is poorly drained. Thus there is a large marshy area between the southern Mackenzie Mountains and Great Slave Lake and a land of innumerable lakes to the east of Great Slave. The frigid northern climate also creates huge stretches of permafrost (ground that is frozen solid to varying depths). Permafrost prevents the growth of deep-rooted vegetation and thus affects both plant and animal life in the north.

The mainland section of the Northwest Territories is mostly, but not entirely, south of the northern limit of wooded country, also known as the tree line. Land north of the tree line is generally tundra, a rolling plain of mosses, lichens, herbs, and dwarf shrubs. In the Northwest Territories, the tree line runs in a southeast direction from where the Mackenzie River empties into the Arctic Ocean. The tree line skirts above Great Bear Lake and Great Slave Lake before plunging south at about the longitude where Saskatchewan and Manitoba meet. A glance at a map shows that the mainland border (starting at Tuktut Nogait National Park) between Northwest Territories and Nunavut roughly follows the northern limit of tree country. This reflects the political intention of making Nunavut a homeland for the Inuit, whose societies have chiefly existed in the inland and coastal areas north of the tree line. All of the Northwest Territories' land in the Arctic archipelago, of course, is well above the tree line.

The Northwest Territories' huge boreal (northern) forest south of the tree line is home to a wide variety of plants and animals. In his journal, Hearne marveled at the diverse wildlife he found upon reaching Great Slave Lake: "[The lake] is full of islands; most of which are clothed with fine tall poplars, birch, and pines, and are well stocked with caribou . . . . On the South side of the lake . . . buffalo, moose, and beaver were very plentiful; and we could discover, in many parts through which we passed, the tracks of martens, foxes, and wolverines and other animals of the furr kind."[3]

■ *Fishermen cruise past a remote cabin on the Mackenzie River.*

■ From Sun Halos to Imaginary Mountains

Beyond being challenging to human life, the extreme weather conditions of the far north can create unusual visual distortions. People in the north have often seen halos around the sun or moon, floating globes apparently coming from the sun, and mountains that are not there. These phenomena do, however, have natural causes.

The halos and floating sun globes, or "sundaes," are caused by ice crystals in the atmosphere. Low-lying clouds in the north, in combination with the sun's low position on the horizon, distort the sun's rays. The denser the cloud layer, the more reflective crystals the cloud has and the brighter the halos and sundaes will be. Sundaes are most common during the spring, and viewers have observed as many as eight balls of light apparently radiating from the sun.

Mirages, such as imaginary mountains or floating ships, are caused by the Arctic's frequent temperature inversions—periods when air close to the ground is colder than overlying air currents. The effect is more common and exaggerated when the days grow longer during the summer months, a period in which sunlight refraction is greater, causing greater distortion.

The forest itself varies widely in the plants and animals it hosts. While much of the territory harbors expansive tracts of evergreen trees, areas near the border with Nunavut have more extensive permafrost. Such permafrost stunts the growth of trees and limits their abundance, leading to the more spotty forests of the north. And because precipitation is so low in many areas, the dry wood is susceptible to frequent forest fires—approximately 1 percent of the Northwest Territories burns each year. Such fires can be environmentally beneficial, however, by clearing the way for new growth.

In transition areas near the tundra, where the permafrost layer extends many feet below the soil's surface, the forest becomes particularly spotty. Large trees are rare, but the ground is carpeted with moss and lichens and dotted with plants such as cranberries, currants, blueberries, and leatherleaf. The red-throated loon, the willow ptarmigan, and the hawk owl are among the various bird species that make their homes in such areas and across the boreal forest.

Touring the Tundra

Above the northern limit of wooded country, the boreal forest gives way to the forbidding tundra. Permafrost in the tundra may begin just four inches below the ground surface. Further, the growing season in the tundra is limited to three months or fewer. The harsh conditions prevent all but the hardiest plant life from surviving.

Even so, the life forms that thrive in the north are striking in their beauty and adaptability. Dwarf willow plants (a low-lying herb, not a tree) cover fields in the relatively more moist river valley areas, which may also host an array of lichens, sedges, and bushes. A number of tundra plants manage to sprout delicate flowers during the short growing season.

As with plants, animal species are limited to those that have managed to adapt to the harsh northern conditions. Arctic foxes and hares, and birds such as sandpipers, gulls, and geese, are common in the tundra. The tundra animal that has probably been the most important to humans is the barren-ground caribou. Caribou live throughout the territory, but the barren-ground herds wander in the tundra along the tree line. They have long been a source of food and clothing for the local Inuit and Dene.

■ *A solitary caribou grazes in a meadow of flowers in northern Northwest Territories.*

The Mighty Mackenzie Mountains

In the southwestern corner of the Northwest Territories, the northernmost extension of the Great Plains of North America yields to the towering Mackenzie Mountains. The Mackenzies themselves are a northern extension of the Rocky Mountain system that runs up the west coast of North America from Mexico to Canada. The mountain range straddles the border of the Northwest Territories and Yukon Territory and lies west of the Mackenzie River.

Rugged and remote, the Mackenzies include the territory's tallest mountain. This officially unnamed peak (climbers refer to it as Mount Nirvana) soars to 9,098 feet (2,773 meters). It is located in the Mackenzie's Ragged Range in the territory's southwest corner, near the border with

■ Viewing the Northern Lights

The northern lights, also known as the aurora borealis, are a spectacular display of rippling bands of colored light often seen in the skies of the far north. The phenomenon can occasionally be observed from points south of the sixtieth parallel—in 1972 people in Miami, Florida, spotted it briefly. The lights are most visible, however, in a narrow band around the so-called auroral oval, the area surrounding the North Magnetic Pole where the northern lights are generated. Because Yellowknife and other places in the Northwest Territories are within this prime viewing band, they have become popular ports of call for fans of the atmospheric show.

The aurora borealis is caused by an interaction of solar wind and the earth's upper atmosphere (ionosphere). Solar wind is gas ejected from the sun's corona, or outer layer. As energized particles speed into space, some enter the earth's ionosphere and are affected by the earth's magnetic field. Scientists believe that when atmospheric oxygen or nitrogen particles that have been "excited" by solar wind return to their normal state, they give off green, red, or purple light.

A number of tours operating out of Yellowknife and Hay River specialize in northern lights viewing. Because the best viewing is when nights are dark enough, usually September through April, these tours often include other winter attractions such as ice fishing, caribou viewing, or snowmobile trips.

■ A 1876 watercolor by artist Thomas Mitchell portrays the aurora borealis at Lady Franklin Bay, Ellesmere Island (now Nunavut).

the Yukon. Nearby, the South Nahanni River begins in the west as a meandering, silt-filled river before plunging abruptly through breathtaking canyons and joining the Liard River in the south.

The Mackenzie Mountains harbor a variety of unique ecosystems and feature some of the unexpected wonders of the territory. Although the upper slopes of mountains are rocky and bare of trees, at lower altitudes and down in the valleys plant growth is plentiful. Tree species such as poplar and birch are common, while black and white spruce and jack pines thrive along the high terraces. Grizzly and black bears, muskrats, minks, martens, beavers, and woodland caribou make their home in the woods, while geese and ducks commonly breed in the area. Less common sightings include trumpeter swans, wolverines, and wood buffalo. A larger and darker-haired cousin to the more populous plains buffalo of points farther south, wood buffalo have recently been reestablished in the Liard River valley area at the southern tip of the Mackenzies. (Curiously, there are no wood buffalo in the Wood Buffalo National Park that Northwest Territories shares with Alberta. The buffalo there are a mixed breed of wood and plains buffalo.)

The Mackenzies are also known for the unusual plants that can be found in the area of various hot springs. Where warm, underground water bubbles to the surface, some plants can thrive well outside of their normal range. For example, hot springs in the Mackenzies support the growth of various species of ferns and orchids that are more commonly found in much warmer climates. One species of orchid seems to be unique to Mackenzie hot springs.

The Territory's Other Mountain Range

The Franklin Mountains, which run some three hundred miles (five hundred kilometers) south to north on the eastern side of the Mackenzie River, offer a subdued contrast to the Mackenzie Mountains. The Franklins do not rival the Mackenzies in height—the tallest peak, Cap Mountain, reaches only some 4,500 feet (1,577 meters)—nor ruggedness. Unlike the rough-hewn Mackenzies, the mountains in the Franklin range are folded, rising in linear ridges above the lowlands around them.

Like the Mackenzie Mountains, however, the Franklin Mountains provide a home to a range of boreal forest plant and animal species. The Franklins are also renowned for the wild rivers, lakes, and canyons found in and around them. The Great Bear River, which cuts through the Franklins from Great Bear Lake, erupts in rapids on its path west to the Mackenzie River. Two small settlements, Deline and Tulita, have been established on both ends of the Great Bear River and are accessible by plane or winter ice roads (temporary roads built each

■ The Great Slave Lake

Located in the south central region of the territories, Great Slave Lake serves as the hub of the Northwest Territories. The territorial capital, Yellowknife, is situated on the lake's North Arm, while Hay River, the second-largest municipality in the territory after Yellowknife, is on the lake's southern shore. Great Slave Lake is also important to people for recreation and employment. For the past fifty years Yellowknife residents have benefited from mining gold and other minerals in the bay and surrounding regions. In addition, tourists and residents alike like to boat and fish on the lake, and many camp on the islands.

The Hay and Slave rivers flow into Great Slave, and the Mackenzie River, the great water highway to the Arctic that is dotted with some of the territory's most remote towns, flows out of it. The huge lake and the surrounding wetlands and plains provide habitat for many of the territory's migratory birds as well as its distinctive wood buffalo.

At 11,172 square miles (28,568 square kilometers), Great Slave is the fifth-largest lake in North America (after three of the Great Lakes, and Great Bear). Both Great Slave and Great Bear are also among the ten largest lakes in the world, measured by both volume and area, while Great Bear is the largest lake on Earth with no road access. Parts of Great Slave plunge to more than two thousand feet (six hundred meters), making it the deepest lake in North America.

■ *In addition to being a prominent recreational attraction, Great Slave Lake is a key habitat for migrating waterfowl.*

winter on frozen rivers, lakes, and swamps). In the northern part of the Franklin range, lakes such as Mahoney near Norman Wells are home to trophy-sized arctic grayling, northern pike, and trout species. In the southern portion of the range, the mountains pass Fish Lake before petering out in the marshy plains that extend far to the west of Great Slave Lake.

The Mackenzie River and Delta

The Mackenzie River drains the eastern slopes of the Mackenzie Mountains and the western slopes of the Franklin Mountains, creating important habitats along its path. The river flows north more than one thousand miles (sixteen hundred kilometers) from Great Slave Lake to the Arctic Ocean's Beaufort Sea. Including its tributaries, the Mackenzie is the second-longest river in North America, after the Mississippi. The Mackenzie is broad and mostly rapid-free. Barges and other boats navigate the river when it is ice-free, usually moving south to north from June to October. The wetlands and forested areas of the river valley support an abundance of plants and animals, including some of the tallest spruce, poplar, and birch trees in the territory. Large mammals found in the area include moose and caribou, grizzly and black bears, and wolves. The affected plain of the river extends on both sides for about 100 miles (160 kilometers) near the Mackenzie's Beaufort Sea outlet.

Near the end of its northward run, the Mackenzie River spreads out into a majestic delta, one of the natural marvels of the territory. The delta is a broad slab of river runoff channels, sand bars, and loose soil. The slow drainage into the Beaufort Sea creates marshes across much of the delta. The islands of the delta are covered in sedges, grasses, herbs such as horsetail, and dwarf shrubs. Small cone-shaped mounds with

■ *Beluga whale meat dries at a whaling station on the Mackenzie River delta near Tuktoyaktuk during the summer of 1955.*

an ice core, known as pingos, dot the landscape. Beluga whales come in from the sea and calve in the Mackenzie River estuary, an area of mixed saltwater and freshwater. Numerous goose species use the delta as a staging area before heading south for the winter, including lesser snow geese, greater white-fronted geese, and black brants.

In addition to hosting so many species, the delta is the site of two small population centers. Approximately one-quarter of the residents of Inuvik, a town of about three thousand, are western Inuit (Inuvialuit). Aklavik, a town of seven hundred, is composed mostly of Inuvialuit and Gwich'in. Aklavik was the main settlement in the area until the 1950s, when the government established Inuvik in a location less prone to flooding and permafrost melting. Some of the residents of Aklavik refused to move, so the town has hung on. Residents of the Mackenzie delta area rely in part on the natural resources around them, including not only the animals and fish that support traditional lifestyles but also the oil and natural gas reserves that support industrial societies.

The Giant Arctic Islands

The Northwest Territories boasts not only two of the largest lakes in the world but also two of the largest islands in the world. At roughly 84,000 square miles (217,000 square kilometers), Victoria Island is the eighth-largest island in the world, about the same size as Great Britain. The western section of Victoria is part of the Northwest Territories, while the eastern and southern parts belong to Nunavut. Banks Island, which lies entirely within the Northwest Territories to Victoria's west, is the twenty-fourth-largest island in the world and is larger than the state of West Virginia. Melville Island (also shared with Nunavut) and Prince Patrick Island are also large enough to dwarf the province of Prince Edward Island.

Although the territory's arctic islands host only two tiny human settlements, the islands include important ecosystems with diverse landforms. Victoria and Banks, separated by the narrow Prince of Wales Strait, lie in the arctic lowland and plateaus region. They do not have permanent ice fields, such as exist on Nunavut's Ellesmere Island to the northeast. Rather their landscapes vary from rolling tundra to river valleys to rocky hills. The few peaks on the territory's arctic islands reach about 2,400 feet (730 meters). The small (population four hundred) town of Holman on the western edge of Victoria shares the huge island with one other settlement, distant Cambridge Bay, Nunavut. The terrain surrounding Holman is tundra with a summer covering of low-growing plants. Musk oxen, which are members of the goat and sheep family, and polar bears are common to the island.

Banks Island just to the west is somewhat similar in its geography. Its terrain ranges from swampy tundra with shallow ponds to valleys of gravel and sand to barren upland plateaus. More than half of the island encompasses two large protected areas, Aulavik National Park and Banks Island Bird Sanctuary No. 1. (Banks Island Bird Sanctuary No. 2 snakes along the Thomsen River, the northernmost canoe-navigable river in North America, within Aulavik.) The protected areas host numerous bird species including oldsquaws, king eider, red phalaropes, tundra swans, and sandhill cranes. According to a recent bird inventory, "75 percent of the bird species (32 out of 43 species) observed in the park are now known to breed there, underscoring the importance of Aulavik as a protected area where a diversity of tundra-adapted birds breed and raise offspring."[4]

In addition to birds, Banks Island is home to perhaps half the world's population of musk oxen. The shaggy beasts may now number as many as seventy thousand, thriving on the dense plant life (which may be increasing from global warming) and the lack of any predators. "Local Inuit fear the herds could soon exceed available grazing lands," writes James Conway, "threatening both the musk-oxen's survival and that of the Peary's caribou that share their environment."[5] Visitors to Banks might also spot wolves, arctic fox, or the occasional polar bear. The only human population center is Sachs Harbour, which, like Holman, is home mostly to a hundred or so Inuit following traditional arctic lifestyles.

Where Whales Outnumber People

The most remote corner of the Northwest Territories includes more islands, most prominently Melville, Prince Patrick, and Mackenzie King. These are large islands—Melville is twice the size of Massachusetts—but they harbor no population centers. Melville has attracted oil and coal prospectors as well as

■ *Musk oxen form a protective circle when threatened by wolves or other predators.*

the occasional team of researchers interested in studying arctic geology or biology.

For the most part the northern islands are bleak and inhospitable to all but the hardiest life forms. The islands north of Banks are surrounded by sea ice year-round. The western section of Melville is more mountainous than the east (which lies in Nunavut) and, like Banks, provides a habitat mainly for musk oxen and various birds. The off-shore waters are important breeding grounds for beluga whales. In addition, bowhead whales live in the Beaufort Sea and are occasionally found near the islands. Orca (killer whales) are also occasional visitors to the Beaufort Sea, where they hunt in packs, sometimes attacking much larger whales. Beyond the whale species, the islands and surrounding seas support walruses, penguins, and seals.

Adapting to the Land

Within the vast expanses of the Northwest Territories are diverse landforms. Across its breadth the territory takes in mountains, rivers, valleys, forests, tundra landscapes, and arctic islands with their icy seas. Numerous plants and animals thrive, though relatively few humans have been willing to adapt to the harsh conditions. Although the human impact on the land thus far has been minimal when compared with much of the rest of Canada, the history of people with close ties to the land of the present-day territory is long and eventful.

The First Peoples and European Exploration

As vast as the Northwest Territories is today, it is much smaller than the area originally known by the name. To the Europeans exploring the New World in the early 1700s, the "north west territory" included virtually all of the land of North America extending west and northwest of the Hudson Bay. Europeans first came in search of the Northwest Passage, and then beaver pelts and other furs.

European newcomers considered this land virgin and unsettled, a place of limitless promise. But of course it had provided a home for aboriginal peoples for thousands of years. While European traders and explorers staked claims to different portions of the territory, opened new markets and established outposts, and changed its official boundaries numerous times over the years, native peoples tried to live much as they had for generations. They had developed small but complex societies well-suited to the challenging conditions of the north. Even so, the onslaught of outsiders brought new technologies, changes in social structures, and varying degrees of prosperity. But natives' interaction with Europeans also brought disaster, including death from disease on unprecedented levels.

The Coastal Inuit

Europeans who first observed how the Inuit live were almost dumbfounded at the difficulties and challenges they faced every day. Raymond de Coccola, a missionary among the Inuit in the 1930s and 1940s, described the lifestyle of a group of people of today's western Nunavut in grim terms: "Freezing and hunger are constant shadows that dog the [Inuit]. This is the main reason they continually wander back and forth across the primeval and cruel Barren Land in an all-consuming search for food. In their desolate homeland of rocks, permafrost, snow, and freezing winds, the odds are heavily loaded in favor of mother nature's vagaries."[6] But the Inuit have a different perspective. They recognize that historically their lifestyles have varied across the polar region and their peoples have not only survived but in many places thrived by adapting to the land and the sea.

Scholars believe that the earliest humans in North America came from Asia at least twelve thousand years ago, and possibly much earlier. They may have crossed a land bridge

■ *An Inuit woman at a summer camp in the Northwest Territories during the early 1950s sews sealskins pegged out to dry.*

that once existed in the Bering Strait. The bands moved south, eventually spreading across North and South America. The first of the truly arctic-dwelling people began to arrive approximately five thousand years ago. Over the centuries, they spread from present-day Alaska across the polar north, stretching all the way to Greenland. The name Inuit now refers to distinct societies that developed north of the tree line some five hundred to one thousand years ago. The Inuit of to-day includes at least eight identifiable tribal groups such as the Caribou Inuit of the western Hudson Bay area and the Inuvialuit of the Mackenzie River delta.

The variations in names hint at greater differences between the groups. De Coccola lived primarily among the central Canadian Inuit groups that lived in igloo houses of snow blocks during the winter and caribou-skin tents during the summer. These inland "Barren Grounds" communities depended on caribou and small game for food, shelter, and clothing. Regional bands typically numbered fewer than fifty people, often of the same family. Elders were respected, and men held unquestioned authority. Cousins and other extended family members acted more like brothers and sisters.

Coastal Inuit groups differed in many respects from inland Inuit and generally enjoyed a much higher standard of living. In addition to hunting large game such as caribou and musk oxen, coastal Inuit took advantage of the abundant resources available from the sea. Seals, whales, and fish gave these Inuit access to more reliable stores of food. Sea mammals in particular were also used to make tools and clothing. While coastal Inuit built ice houses for food storage, and for shelter during seal hunts on sea ice, they lived year-round in villages often consisting of several single-family and multi-family houses. These were typically log-and-sod houses dug partially into the ground for warmth. Nations numbered anywhere between a few hundred to nearly a thousand people. A powerful male typically headed extended families of up to fifty members.

The tribal group that existed in the Mackenzie delta area until the end of the nineteenth century was known as the Mackenzie Inuit. They numbered about twenty-five hundred people, or roughly as many as all the Inuit living between them and the Hudson Bay. With their powerful villages and families, they regarded themselves as superior to the rest of the Inuit.

■ Hunting the Mammoths of the Ocean

Coastal Inuit groups hunted mainly two types of whale, the large bowhead whale and the much smaller beluga whale. For each, the Inuit developed hunting techniques that are still in use among some of their people today. The hunt for whales typically began in the spring when seasonal sea ice began to break up. Hunters in single-manned boats or in larger boats pulled up onto a platform of ice and waited for a whale to surface. This waiting period could last days or even weeks. Once a whale surfaced, the hunters gave chase in their boats. When they got close enough, a hunter plunged a harpoon strung with ropes into the whale. Inflated seal-skin bags attached to the harpoon ropes floated, thereby both marking the whale's position for the hunters and tiring the escaping whale. After pursuing the whale until it was exhausted, the hunters speared it repeatedly with stone-tipped lances until the animal died. They then hauled the whale onto shore using seal-skin ropes, butchered it, and took the meat and other useful parts back to their families.

For smaller beluga whales, the Inuit strung together seal-skin nets near the shores. When small whales became entangled in the nets, hunters went out to the whales and speared them until they died. The hunters then brought the whales to shore for butchering.

■ *Two Inuvialuit hunters in a canoe troll the southern Artic Ocean for white whales.*

The Forest-Dwelling Dene

The Mackenzie Inuit were distinct not only from their Inuit cousins to the east but also from their forest-dwelling neighbors to the south, the Dene. The Dene are as diverse as the Inuit, comprising at the time of European exploration groups such as the Dogrib (now Tlicho, pronounced tlee-chon) who lived south of Great Bear Lake, the Kutchin (now Gwich'in) of the northern Mackenzie River area, and the Yellowknive and Slavey of the Great Slave Lake area. These and other Dene societies have developed over thousands of years in boreal forest areas, and the North American Dene have close relatives in Russia and northern Asia. Most Dene speak a variation on the Athapaskan languages common to aboriginal groups in the area of the present-day territory and northern Alberta and Saskatchewan. Many tribes shared the Mackenzie River, which they call the Deh Cho ("big river"), for transport and for food.

Like the Inuit, the Dene differ from group to group, though they share many commonalities, as well. The Dene were skilled hunters. Near the present-day border of Alberta, they relied on buffalo, beaver, and woodland caribou for food and other necessities. In the north near Great Bear Lake, the First Nations relied on moose, woodland and barren-ground caribou, Dall's sheep, beaver, marten, muskrats, and birds for their food. The caribou was particularly important since it provided meat, furs for clothing and shelter, sinew for sewing, and antlers and bones for tools.

The Dene differed in lifestyle and social structure from group to group. The Slavey were generally a peaceable people. They shared a common language but tended not to organize

■ *A native woman in the Fort Resolution area engages in a rite of spring: the tapping of birch trees for their sap.*

around central authority figures. Rather, they roamed in family-related groups of up to thirty individuals during the winter, hunting moose, caribou, and small game. In the summer, bands grouped together, often on a lake, and hunted, foraged for berries, and fished.

The Gwich'in, the northernmost group of the Dene, were also nomadic. They relied heavily on caribou for food and shelter during the fall, but their survival often depended on Mackenzie River fish spawning in the spring. Their need for food during the various seasons took them all over the Mackenzie River valley and delta area in the north. Their homes were temporary and built of unique materials. Skin- and bark-covered, domed dwellings have been found in some places, but more substantial homes of poles and sod have also been found. The best known type, though, among the Gwich'in was a moss house, or *nynkun,* that temporarily housed a hunter in search of caribou or other forest game. The Gwich'in, like other Dene groups, were enemies of the Inuit and had regular conflicts with them.

For both the Inuit and the Dene, their traditional lifestyles generally suited them for centuries. But the coming of Europeans vastly changed their economies and their way of life.

The First European Explorers

British sailors in search of a Northwest Passage to China were the earliest Europeans to explore the frozen northern stretches of North America. Martin Frobisher was the first to arrive in the subarctic north, claiming today's Baffin Island in present-day Nunavut for England in 1577. In the late 1580s, John Davis entered the huge bay, now known as Baffin Bay, between present-day Greenland and arctic Canada. Between 1610 and 1611 Henry Hudson explored the bay later named for him, and he was followed by expeditions led by Thomas Button in 1612 and Thomas James in 1631. In general these sailors came ashore only for short periods and did not explore inland. It was not until the early 1690s that fur trader Henry Kelsey ventured up the Hayes River from the Hudson Bay, eventually reaching present-day Saskatchewan. The journeys of these British explorers never reached as far as present-day Northwest Territories, but they did chart new territory and open the way for increased commerce with northern native peoples.

The first European to enter the present-day Northwest Territories may have been another fur trader, William Stuart.

In 1715 he headed northwest from Fort York, on the western shores of Hudson Bay, with a large party and a Chipewyan guide, Thanadelthur, who also spoke Cree. Stuart's main mission was to reestablish peace between warring tribes of Cree and Chipewyan and thus promote the fur trade with his employer, the Hudson's Bay Company. He probably traveled past the present-day boundary between Northwest Territories and Nunavut, but unfortunately he did not create journals or maps that could establish exactly where he had been.

Certainly the first European to reach the Great Slave Lake was the Hudson's Bay Company trader Samuel Hearne. He too was guided by a Chipewyan in an expedition that set out from Fort Prince of Wales (near present-day Churchill, Manitoba) on Hudson Bay in late 1770. Hearne and his companions headed inland in search of copper mines, the Northwest Passage, and expanded trade routes. They traversed the region known as the barren lands of present-day Nunavut and reached Coronation Gulf south of Victoria Island. The expedition then moved south along the Coppermine River, arrived at the Great Slave Lake in December 1771, and returned to the Hudson Bay in June 1772. Hearne started with few supplies and consequently relied on friendly native peoples along the way to help him find food and manage the treacherous conditions. Hunger and frigid temperatures haunted his two-year exploration, and he saw some around him die. He grimly records the passing of a native woman near the Great Slave Lake:

■ *London-born explorer and fur trader Samuel Hearne (1745–1792) wrote vivid descriptions of his travels in northern Canada.*

> One of the Indian's wives, who for some time had been in a consumption, had become so weak as to be incapable of traveling. . . . Without much ceremony, she was left unassisted, to perish above-ground. . . . Sometimes persons thus left, recover; and come up with their friends. Instances of this kind are seldom known. The poor woman above mentioned, however, came up with us several times. At length, poor creature! she dropt behind, and no one attempted to go back in search of her.[7]

In some ways, Hearne's mission was unsuccessful. He found no river route that could be part of a Northwest Passage; the copper mines were disappointing; and the topographical maps he drew were inaccurate. But, for better or worse, Hearne opened the area to further European exploration, and his cooperation with native peoples along the way encouraged others to seek out native peoples to partner with in their explorations and trade.

Alexander Mackenzie's River Journey

The Scottish-born fur trader Alexander Mackenzie was the next most important European explorer to venture into the wilderness of the far northwest. Like Hearne before him, he was driven to find new rivers that could expand trade routes across the continent. In the mid-1780s, Mackenzie was one of the founders of the North West Company, a fur-trading outfit that quickly set out to rival the well-established Hudson's Bay Company. Mackenzie was posted to Fort Chipewyan on the western shores of Lake Athabasca (present-day Alberta) and charged with exploring new areas and seeking out new peoples to trade with. At Fort Chipewyan he met veteran fur trader Peter Pond, who was convinced that there was a great river route from that part of the country all the way to the Pacific Ocean.

In 1786 Pond had established Old Fort Providence on the banks of the Great Slave Lake, near where the Yellowknife River enters the lake's North Arm. (Another Fort Providence was built almost a century later far to the south on the Mackenzie River; it evolved into the present-day town of Fort Providence.) Pond convinced Mackenzie that the great river running west out of the southwestern part of Great Slave Lake was a route to the Pacific, and in 1789 Mackenzie organized an expedition to explore the river. He visited Old Fort Providence en route before traveling the length of the Dene's Deh Cho, which to Mackenzie's and Pond's disappointment ran not west to the Pacific but north to the Arctic Ocean.

Mackenzie's small party of explorers on the three-month expedition to the Beaufort Sea and back included a number of natives. His reliance on their knowledge and skills reflected the evolving relationship between Europeans and aboriginals. Mackenzie alternately bribed his native contacts with trade promises and alcohol and threatened them in order to keep his expedition intact. He later acknowledged the native people's help in taking the journey to its successful (although disappointing) conclusion, but the underlying tensions hinted at problems that would soon befall the Dene and the Inuit. Dene leader Stephen Kakfwi, who was elected the territory's premier in 2000, said of Mackenzie,

> Alexander Mackenzie came to our land. He described us in his Journal as a 'meagre, ill-made people . . . people with scabby legs.' My people probably wondered at this strange, pale man in his ridiculous clothes, asking about some great waters he was searching for. He recorded his views on the people, but we'll never know exactly how my people saw him. I know they'd never understand why their river is named after such an insignificant fellow.[8]

Mackenzie's exploration of the river later named for him (the Mackenzie Mountains, on the other hand, are named for another famous Alexander Mackenzie, Canada's second prime minister) charted new territory for Europeans and opened trade even farther westward and northward. While Mackenzie had failed to find a river that would lead to the Pacific (a subsequent 1793 journey along the Peace and other rivers did reach the Pacific), he nevertheless made excellent topographical maps that aided further exploration and heightened the pace of trade. Explorers such as John Franklin who followed in his footsteps benefited from his maps and pushed the area's frontiers to the far reaches of the continent.

 Alexander Mackenzie (1764–1820) called the river now named after him "the River of Disappointment" when it took him to the Arctic Ocean rather than to the Pacific.

Trouble in the Fur Trade

The expeditions of Hearne, Mackenzie, and others gradually opened the area to trade. The native peoples became accustomed to exchanging meat, furs, trinkets, and other goods at places such as Fort Resolution on Great Slave Lake, Fort

■ The Final Expedition of John Franklin

Alexander Mackenzie's explorations above the Arctic Circle inspired others to follow. Among the most determined nineteenth-century arctic explorers was John Franklin, who led three expeditions to the area over a span of more than twenty-five years. On trips to the Canadian Arctic in 1819, 1825, and 1845 he explored islands and seaways, ventured inland across Great Bear Lake, and mapped over twenty-five hundred miles (four thousand kilometers) of arctic coastline. His work provided the most accurate view of the far north of the time, but his final journey ended in tragedy.

Franklin's fateful expedition aboard two ships, the *Erebus* and the *Terror*, left England in May 1845. The sailors hoped to become the first to successfully navigate the Northwest Passage. Franklin and his men reached Lancaster Sound, across the Baffin Bay from Greenland, in present-day Nunavut, in July. Over the next year the 129-man expedition sailed around Cornwallis Island, wintered on nearby Beechey Island, and then started south. The ships apparently became stuck in ice near King William Island, however, and never went any farther.

When Franklin's ships failed to return to England, the British and American governments, the Hudson's Bay Company, and even Franklin's wife organized search parties. Beginning in 1848, dozens of expeditions were launched to find the lost explorers. An 1854 party led by captain John Rae finally learned the awful truth, by talking to local Inuit and finding personal effects of sailors on King William Island. A note left in a cairn (a stone monument) at Victory Point on the island established that Franklin died there,

Franklin on Great Bear Lake, and at Fort Simpson and other forts along the Mackenzie River. Initially, this expanding fur trade was a boon to native peoples. They profited by acting as guides for European explorations and benefited from using some of the goods they traded for.

The fur-based economy that had long dominated the area of "Rupert's Land," the huge area of Hudson Bay drainage originally granted to the Hudson's Bay Company in 1670, ultimately would prove to be unstable. In 1821, the North West Company merged with the Hudson's Bay Company and ended the rivalry that had driven the two companies to deeper reaches of the continent and to heightened violence. The seemingly insatiable demand for beaver furs, which were used aged sixty, on June 11, 1847. The remaining officers and crew (three had perished on Beechey) spent the summer of 1847 aboard the ship, hoping it would free itself from the ice. When the ice failed to melt, the men spent a second terrible winter on the ship. In late April 1848, the 105 men still alive abandoned the ship to trek overland, hoping to get off the island and presumably head south for the Hudson Bay. None of the crew was ever found alive, nor were the ships ever discovered.

Exactly what happened to most of Franklin's crew, and why the mission failed so abysmally, has been a mystery ever since. Even after Rae's findings, numerous other expeditions have searched for evidence of the ships or crew. The research has extended to recent times—during the early 1990s researchers found human skeletal remains on King William that are thought to be from the Franklin expedition. Bone analysis suggests that the crew faced dangers from more than the freezing weather and lack of food. The sailors apparently suffered from scurvy, due to lack of vitamin C, and from lead poisoning, due to eating food from lead-soldered cans. The bones also showed that some sailors resorted to cannibalism.

As for the Northwest Passage, Franklin's expedition is credited with finding a key passageway, the Peel Sound between Somerset and Prince of Wales islands. Even so, it would not be until Norwegian Roald Amundsen's 1903 journey on the *Gjoa* that a ship would successfully navigate the entire length of the Northwest Passage—and even the *Gjoa* spent one winter trapped in ice.

to make popular hats and other garments in Europe, enriched the native peoples in the short term. Over time, however, the fur trade led to the development of settlements that radically changed the daily lives of the native peoples.

In the mid-nineteenth century, the fur trade began a gradual decline. European fashions changed, reducing the demand for beaver pelts. Over-trapping of beaver started to deplete the stocks of these animals. In the area to the south of Great Slave Lake, the plains buffalo and its larger cousin, the wood buffalo, also began to disappear. By the 1880s, they were nearly extinct. In the mixed woodlands between Great Slave and Great Bear, the barren-ground and woodland caribou suffered huge depletions. Native tribes were forced to search farther afield from their traditional hunting grounds. In many cases, native peoples had to settle for smaller game that did not yield the plentiful resources larger animals had traditionally provided.

Changes for the Inuit

The push north had profound effects on the Inuit as well. Initially, Europeans who met the Inuit had minimal interaction with them. Europeans often saw little value in the Inuit's skills and insights. (Franklin's arrogance may have doomed his final expedition; if he had been less aloof from natives, he might have been able to heed their warnings and learn from their survival skills.) The Inuit also did not have goods that most Europeans valued as trade items.

In many respects, the Inuit remained aloof, as well. The Mackenzie Inuit, for example, initially steered clear of the first fort in their vicinity, Peel's River Post (later called Fort Mc-Pherson), established in the 1840s on the Peel River. Eventually the Mackenzie Inuit did venture into the fort to trade fox and other pelts for metal fish hooks and pots, glass beads, iron knives, and tobacco.

As their interactions with the Inuit increased, Europeans found the Inuit to be highly skilled in northern survival, hunting, and trade. For the Inuit of the Mackenzie River delta, change was somewhat slower in coming than it was to other Inuit. In the early 1860s the Hudson's Bay Company opened Fort Anderson on the Anderson River to the east of the Mackenzie River delta to specifically target the Inuit. Eventually, Europeans drew the native peoples into trade, which temporarily proved profitable for all involved. But European diseases began to spread among the natives, and the Europeans ultimately closed Fort Anderson because of poor profits. The fort closure hurt the Inuit economy, and with their numbers decreasing due to disease, many began to marry into other Inuit groups.

Meanwhile, European whalers had struck up relationships with other Inuit groups. This trading relationship increased in the 1850s when demand for whale blubber and whale products shot up around the world. Europeans hired hundreds of Inuit to work on whaling ships in jobs ranging from harpooners to seamstresses. Europeans, with the help of the Inuit and their skillful whaling techniques, killed thousands of whales. The number of bowheads and other whales decreased at a frightening pace, much like the near-extinction of buffalo. By 1905, with whale populations decimated, world demand for whale oil fell in favor of petroleum products. The depletion of the caribou stock hurt the Inuit, as well. The Inuit were left without some of their most important resources.

European Diseases Menace Natives

Even more devastating than the loss of crucial animals for the Inuit were the diseases the Europeans brought with them to the New World. Not having been exposed to these diseases (many of which could ultimately be traced to European livestock) over many centuries, as the Europeans were, native peoples had not developed any natural immunity. Diseases that Europeans usually survived, like measles, could be fatal to high percentages of natives. At least twenty-eight Inuit, for example, died from measles in the vicinity of Fort Anderson in 1865. Inuit anger over this episode was one of the reasons why the Hudson's Bay Company closed Fort Anderson in 1866.

Smallpox was more deadly to the Inuit. Year after year, smallpox epidemics depleted the Inuit population. "We are all dying, we are getting snuffed out day by day,"[9] one chief said in the 1870s. Smallpox and dysentery caused the Mackenzie Inuit population to fall from 2,500 in 1850 to just 150 in 1910. So few Mackenzie Inuit survived that Inuit from northern Alaska to the west gradually moved into the delta area and took over. It is these western Inuit, or Inuvialuit, who dominate the delta area today.

Other Inuit tribal groups were wiped out altogether, most notably the Sadlermiuts of Coats and other islands in the northern reaches of Hudson Bay. They became extinct as a people when a disease (either typhus or typhoid) brought ashore from a whaling ship in the fall of 1902 killed all of the remaining seventy or so Sadlermiuts.

Dene groups suffered similarly. Even on some of Alexander Mackenzie's early journeys, he recorded that natives were experiencing severe effects from European illnesses. By the 1900s, a number of tribes had lost as many as 90 percent of

■ The Evolution of the Northwest Territories

The boundaries and indeed even the name of today's Northwest Territories have changed many times over the centuries. In 1670, England's King Charles II gave the Hudson's Bay Company a charter to trade in Rupert's Land. This included approximately half of present-day Canada, from Labrador all the way to southern Alberta. Fur traders and others eventually began to use "the north west territory" to refer loosely to all the land north and west of Lake Superior.

In 1859 the British "Indian Territories Act" created the North-Western Territory, basically the land west of Rupert's Land and north of the then newly created west coast colony of British Columbia. This territory included all of present-day Yukon Territory as well as parts of today's Alberta, Saskatchewan, Northwest Territories, and Nunavut. In 1870, the new dominion of Canada purchased Rupert's Land from the Hudson's Bay Company and folded it into a massive North-West Territories. At the time, the new provinces of Ontario, Quebec, and Manitoba were much smaller than they are at present, so the North-West Territories spanned an area comparable in size to today's continental United States.

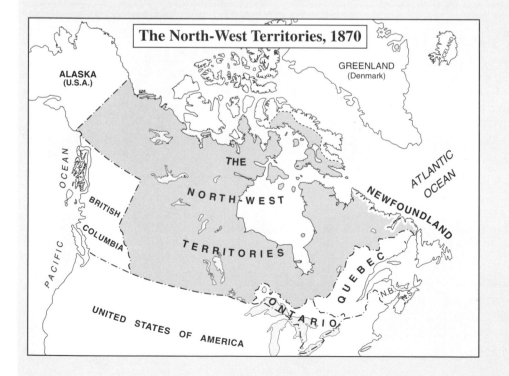

The Arctic Ocean islands north of the Canadian mainland were not part of the North-West Territories until the British government transferred its arctic island possessions to Canada in 1880. The issue of arctic sovereignty, however, was hardly settled—other countries, particularly Norway and the United States, had interests in these islands and legal claims that were, at least initially, even stronger than Canada's. Over the next fifty years, Canada's explorations and settlements slowly established its rights to all of the arctic islands north of its mainland and west of Greenland.

As the North-West Territories grew to the north, its mainland area shrank as Canada carved out new provinces (Manitoba in 1881, and Alberta and Saskatchewan in 1905) and a territory (Yukon in 1898). In the early years of the twentieth century, Canada extended the borders of Manitoba, Ontario, and Quebec northward, further reducing the territory's land, and dropped the hyphen from "north-west." The Northwest Territories reached its present configuration when Nunavut was officially created in 1999.

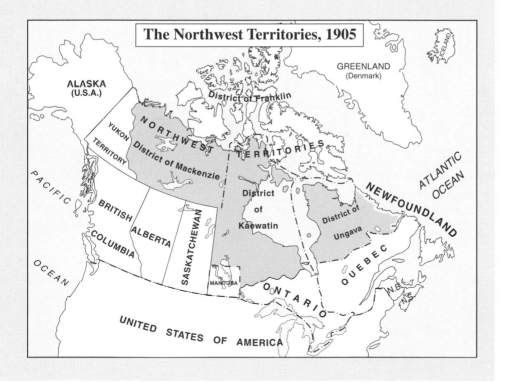

The Northwest Territories, 1905

their members to smallpox and other diseases. With their numbers decimated and their buffalo and caribou stocks depleted, various Dene First Nations were compelled to sign treaties with the Canadian government between 1899 and 1921. The treaties guaranteed certain lands to the Dene, but forever altered their existence.

CHAPTER 3

Toward the Twentieth Century

Until the first half of the twentieth century, relatively few Europeans had filtered into the area of the present-day Northwest Territories, and the handful that did live there were generally traders in small outposts. But from 1870 on, the seemingly small European contingent profoundly shaped the area's government, economy, and society. Native peoples found themselves subject to the new Canadian government, a body that they generally had little to do with and in which they had no representation. Meanwhile, pioneering groups of Canadian miners and settlers made their way north, first to the gold found in the Yukon and later to the mineral riches available within the Northwest Territories. Although Canadian settlement of the far north was sporadic, the newcomers shared little in common with the native peoples who had been living there for hundreds or even thousands of years. Many of the inevitable disagreements and differences between the settlers and the natives persist to this day.

The Rule from Afar

In 1867 the four British colonies of Ontario, Quebec, New Brunswick, and Nova Scotia collectively won their independence from England. (A fifth colony, Newfoundland, rejected confederation and remained semi-independent until 1949.) The new country of Canada immediately faced a number of thorny challenges, including what to do about the huge tracts of land surrounding the Hudson Bay that were still controlled by the Hudson's Bay Company. Within three years, Canada had forged an agreement with the company to purchase the land, officially dubbed the North-West Territories in 1870.

During its early history the huge territory was governed by a lieutenant governor and a legislative council appointed by officials in Ottawa, Canada's national capital. Between 1870 and 1905, Canada modified the territory's administrative structure a number of times while essentially preserving federal control. Even after the creation of Saskatchewan and Alberta in 1905, when the federal government arranged for the territory to be ruled by a commission of senior officials and a federally appointed commissioner, most of the political power remained in Ottawa.

Control by a distant government had mostly negative effects on the native peoples of the area. Lacking political power, First Nations were unable to reestablish their once-independent cultures. Between 1871 and 1921, the federal government and various northern and Great Plains tribes signed a series of eleven separate treaties. Most of these treaties promised native peoples certain amounts of money, reserve land, and social services (such as education) in exchange for control of large chunks of the territory and the right to use land for mineral exploitation, settlement, and transportation. These treaties were one-sided in favor of the Canadian government, but the First Nations felt they had no option but to sign. In 1880 Roderick MacFarlane, a government officer at Fort Chipewyan, described the situation of native peoples living in the area from his post to the Mackenzie River:

> Owing to the scarcity of food animals, and the comparative failure of the fisheries, numbers of Indians will doubtless suffer many privations betwixt [now] and Spring. . . . It strikes me very forcibly that something must be done and that speedily to help these poor people. Confining my remarks as applicable to the District of Peace River, Athabasca, English River, and the Mackenzie, I am really unaware of anything that has yet been accomplished by our rulers . . . since the territory was transferred to Canada.[10]

As MacFarlane noted, the native peoples were impoverished and starving, the stocks of their traditional food sources were being depleted, and the government was doing little to help. The policy of the government was that there would be no help without a treaty. By 1921, almost all of the tribes native to the area of present-day Northwest Territories had signed, including the North Slavey, the Dogrib, and the Gwich'in.

Post-Treaty Problems

The treaties generally failed to improve the lot of the native peoples. The government wanted tribes to become industrious farmers, and treaties even promised agricultural equipment and livestock. But many native peoples had little experience in farming, having developed over centuries of time into nomadic, hunting-gathering societies. Making a quick transition to a farming lifestyle was difficult, at best, for those who attempted it, necessitating as it did radical changes in diet, work roles, tools, and virtually every other aspect of everyday culture. Moreover, many of the reserve lands were too arid or too far north to be profitably farmed. Poverty and social problems prevailed throughout the twentieth century on most reserves.

In addition, the treaties themselves meant something different to native peoples and left open issues that persist to the present day. Native leaders saw the agreements as promises of peace, cooperation, and friendship, rather than as documents that ended native land entitlements. With this fundamental misunderstanding, native peoples resented the government that, they believed, had unjustly restricted them to specific lands for their use.

Missionaries and the Government Among the Inuit

While the Inuit did not enter into any of the signed treaties, their cultures were also greatly affected by developments in the late nineteenth century. Perhaps chief among these was the arrival of Christian missionaries. The Christian missionaries that accompanied the first whalers had converted virtually no Inuit, but the Anglican and Catholic missionaries that came in the 1890s and stayed through the turn of the century had a greater effect. At various places across the northern parts of today's Northwest Territories and Nunavut, religious leaders set up small congregations of twenty to thirty people.

■ *Inuvik's igloo-inspired Church of Our Lady of Victory is a Catholic house of worship that was built in 1958.*

Among the Inuvialuit, the first baptism occurred in 1909. The missionaries' culture tended to suppress ancient Inuit beliefs and traditions. Many Inuit practices were kept privately or disappeared altogether.

In the meantime, the fur trade extended north to the Inuit, and with it came the Royal Canadian Mounted Police, the police arm of the government. By the early 1930s, the Canadian government had solidified its legal claim to the arctic islands between the mainland and the North Pole, thus effectively putting almost all of North America's Inuit cultures under Canadian power. Much like the First Nations to the south, the Inuit found themselves at the political mercy of a government thousands of miles away and at the economic mercy of fur retailers in far away London and New York. The result was an increase of poverty, despair, and social problems among the Inuit.

The Allure of Gold

Until the 1920s and 1930s, the Northwest Territories was still sparsely populated. The 1910 census showed only seventeen

■ The Residential Schools Scandal

One of the unfortunate legacies of early missionary work among First Nation tribes is the infamous "residential schools" system that existed in Canada during much of the nineteenth and twentieth centuries. Concurrent with European settlement of frontier areas, Roman Catholic, Anglican, Presbyterian, and other religious orders began to organize schools that displaced young natives from their families and societies, often for years at a time. The natives were taught "white ways" so that they could be more quickly integrated into conventional Canadian/European culture. When the Canadian government began signing treaties with First Nation tribes in the 1870s, it started to operate many of these residential schools in cooperation with the churches.

Some 130 residential schools operated throughout much of Canada, including nine in present-day Northwest Territories. The residential schools imposed strict discipline on students, restricted the use of native languages in favor of English, and forced new religious beliefs on the children. In addition, in as many as one hundred of the schools, teachers and administrators physically and sometimes sexually abused the students.

The federal government took total control over the residential schools in 1969, closing most by the end of the 1970s and the last one in 1996. Within the past decade, however, First Nations and the Canadian government have begun to acknowledge, and attempt to repair, the considerable damage the residential schools program caused, both to individuals and to native culture in general. A number of studies and commissions have substantiated widespread abuse in the schools. According to Indian Residential Schools Resolution Canada, a program the Canadian government has established to deal with the issue, "In addition to allegations of physical and sexual abuse, which are found in 90% of the legal claims, allegations [relate] to such things as cultural loss, breach of treaty, loss of education opportunity, forcible confinement and poor conditions at the schools."

First Nations peoples have filed some five thousand suits in various courts, seeking redress (from churches and the government) for twelve thousand individuals who suffered physical or emotional harm while attending the schools. The government has also filed criminal charges in a number of places. For example, three persons employed during the 1960s and 1970s at Inuvik's Grollier Hall residential school were charged with indecent assault and other sexual offenses against twenty-five victims. The men were convicted in 1998 and sentenced to prison.

thousand people in the area enclosed today by the Northwest Territories and Nunavut. Of those, about sixteen thousand were aboriginals, approximately five hundred were of British descent, and roughly two hundred were French. Today, by contrast, the population of the Northwest Territories is split more or less evenly between whites and natives. (Inuit constitute a strong majority in Nunavut.) The influx of non-aboriginals into present-day Northwest Territories is a story of minerals and of the dream of gold and riches in the far north.

A hint of the population changes that would come occurred during the late 1890s when prospectors found gold near the Klondike River, in the far west of the Northwest Territories. Most of the thousands of gold diggers who quickly struck out for the Klondike reached it by taking a steamer to Skagway, Alaska. From there, they faced a difficult but relatively short trek over the coastal mountains and then a long but not especially arduous float down the Yukon River.

Fifteen hundred or so hardy souls also tried to reach the Klondike from the east, along the so-called "All-Canadian Route" that took off from Edmonton in present-day Alberta. This was primarily a river route, down the Athabasca, Slave, and Mackenzie Rivers almost to the Arctic Ocean and then overland to the Yukon. Although few who set out made it all the way to the Klondike, some of those who did not ended up staying in parts of the Northwest Territories. A few prospectors even managed to find gold on the shores of the Great Slave Lake. Their strike, however, failed to trigger a Klondike-like gold rush. The gold seemed not as plentiful, nor as accessible, as in the Klondike. Also, although the Great Slave Lake is farther south of the Arctic Circle than the Klondike, it is equally if not more remote. The need for hardcore wilderness survival and travel skills while making the overland and river route to the Great Slave Lake prevented hordes of roughnecks from swamping the area.

The gold fever of the 1890s had a number of long-term effects on the remote territory. For one, the influx of people and the need for keeping law and order in the Klondike led Canada to carve the new Yukon Territory from the Northwest Territories. The miners and others who came north, whether temporarily or permanently, increased contacts with aboriginals. The mining also opened government officials' eyes to the north as a region of economic opportunity should the transportation difficulties ever be overcome.

Airplanes and Miners Arrive

The Northwest Territories experienced its next period of rapid change when two developments came together in the 1930s. The first of these was the advent of reliable air travel, since the territory was still relatively inaccessible by overland travel. The Northwest Territories did not have a single vehicle in it until 1920, and it would be another four decades after that before a highway connected Yellowknife to Edmonton, more than nine hundred miles (fifteen hundred kilometers) to the south. Even today only two additional highways, neither of which is paved, link the territory to points south. Air travel offered an alternative way for people and supplies to reach the far north.

Of particular importance was the development of seaplanes that could land and take off on water, including floatplanes (which have water-tight pontoons attached by struts to the fuselage) and flying boats (which can land and float on the fuselage itself). The first practical seaplane was invented by American Glenn Curtiss in 1911, but a number of Canadian aviators and airplane builders helped to make seaplanes some of the biggest and fastest flying machines of the 1920s. Seaplanes were perfect for getting around the lake-strewn Canadian north, where landing strips were rarer than a hot day in January. Skis replaced pontoons in the winter to allow bush pilots to land on frozen lakes and rivers.

■ *The Hudson's Bay Company operated this Beechcraft floatplane out of Yellowknife in the late 1930s.*

The second crucial development was the discovery of commercial minerals. In 1930, bush pilot Clennell Dickins, a former World War I pilot, flew prospector and mining promoter Gilbert Labine over the eastern shores of Great Bear Lake. Labine's keen eye for minerals allowed him to spot a deposit of pitchblende, a heavy, brown to black mineral. In 1898 Marie and Pierre Curie had extracted the radioactive element radium from pitchblende. By the late 1920s, radium was being recognized as a useful tool in cancer therapy. Labine eventually established the Eldorado Mining & Refining company at the Great Bear Lake site as well as a radium refinery at Port Hope, Ontario.

The pitchblende mining that Labine soon had underway rekindled interest in the Great Slave Lake area as a potential source of minerals, especially gold. In 1934 a Geological Survey of Canada team identified a seam of gold in Yellowknife Bay. This touched off a gold rush that may not have quite rivaled that of late-1890s Yukon but was nevertheless frenzied. Prospectors put up a ragtag tent camp on a small peninsula in the Bay. Within two years, this camp had turned into the boomtown of Yellowknife.

City of Yellow Metals

Yellowknife may sound like it was named for gold, but the name is actually traced to another yellowish mineral: copper. When John Franklin's 1820 inland expedition reached the Great Slave Lake, it encountered a Dene tribe that used copper-bladed knives. To the Europeans, the tribe became the Yellowknives, and a small trading post that was started on the banks of the North Arm of the Great Slave Lake was known as Yellowknife. Other tribes subsequently occupied the area of the Great Slave Lake, such as today's Slavey and Yellowknife Chipewyan. (The original Yellowknives no longer exist, having either died off or been dispersed into other tribes.) Until the gold strike of 1934, Yellowknife remained a tiny native post in a sparsely populated wilderness.

While the new mineral industry spurred the growth of mining towns and settlements on Great Slave and Great Bear lakes, Yellowknife quickly began to outstrip rivals as the commercial capital of the territory. The Consolidated Mining and Smelting Company of Canada (Cominco) staked a claim in Yellowknife and hired workers to sink shafts, excavate tunnels, and build mills to extract the gold from the ore. One Cominco

■ The Secret A-Bomb History of Great Bear Lake

Until 1940, uranium was generally considered a useless byproduct of radium production. In March of that year, the Canadian nuclear physicist George Laurence began to use uranium in nuclear fission experiments he was conducting at the National Research Council of Canada in Ottawa. With World War II under way, Laurence and other Canadian and British scientists were in the initial stages of experiments that would soon establish the potential for radioactive elements such as uranium to be used to make atomic weapons. In December 1941 the United States entered the war, and in August 1942 it officially organized the Manhattan Project to attempt to build the first atomic bomb. Nuclear physicists from various Allied nations gathered at a secret facility in Los Alamos, New Mexico, to undertake the complex weapons project.

The researchers soon realized that a concentrated supply of uranium would be essential for success. At the time, there were only two potential sources for large amounts of uranium ore: a mine in Africa and Labine's mine on Great Bear Lake. In 1942, the Canadian government quietly bought Labine's mine and used it to supply the Manhattan Project with the necessary uranium. Scientists successfully detonated the first atomic bomb in the desert of Socorro County, New Mexico, on July 16, 1945.

"When World War II ended," scholar D. McCormack Smyth has noted, "Canada had all the resources necessary to become a powerful nuclear weapons state. It had the uranium, its scientists knew how to release the power of the atom, and its engineers and technical experts knew how to build and operate the equipment to do it. But Canada consciously decided that it would not be a nuclear weapons state."

mine, the so-called Con Mine, was producing enough gold by 1938 to pour the company's first gold bricks.

The commercial production of gold, which began in earnest with Cominco's first extraction, triggered explosive growth and organization in Yellowknife. In 1939, territory officials created the Yellowknife Administration District. By the following year the population had reached one thousand, and Yellowknife was a ramshackle array of wooden cabins on the rocky shores.

World War II had a definite cooling effect, however, on the growing town. Two of Yellowknife's six gold mines closed in 1942, and by 1944, production in all mines had ceased. The

■ *The Con Mine, shown here in 1939, has long been a dominant force in Yellowknife's economy.*

war effort required the men who worked the mines to leave for other industries. Furthermore, gold was not an important war resource, so its market value dropped steeply during war time.

A New Territorial Capital

Yellowknife underwent a resurgence when World War II ended. The Con Mine reopened, and in 1948 a second major gold mine within city limits, the Giant Mine, began operations. The success of these large mines attracted prospectors and mining operations to Yellowknife as well as to the remote country north of the town. Most of the small companies, notes local historian Ryan Silke, "Despite their scheming and market manipulations never found much gold."[11] The Con and Giant mines, however, became two of the most productive gold mines in Canada, sinking shafts more than six thousand feet (eighteen hundred meters) deep and carving tunnels beneath both city and bay. Yellowknife became "the city built on gold," and the territory increased in stature on the national scene.

Yellowknife's burgeoning population soon outgrew the Old Town peninsula, the site of the original tent camp. Planners surveyed a "New Town" site on the shore of Great Slave Lake and began construction on it in 1947. A hydroelectric plant built in 1948 harnessed power from the nearby Snare River and allowed for steady growth for the next several decades. In 1953 Yellowknife became a municipal district and elected its first mayor. In 1967, it became the official capital of the Northwest Territories, much to the dismay of Fort Smith, which had long served as unofficial capital of the north. (Regina was the capital of the Northwest Territories from 1883 until 1905, when it became the capital of the new province of Saskatchewan. From 1905 until 1967, the Northwest Territories had no capital—its seat of government was officially Ottawa.)

The Con and Giant mines have been owned by Miramar Mining Corporation since 1999 and remain in operation as of early 2003. By historic standards the two mines are among the top dozen gold-producing mines in the world, having yielded between them more than 14 million ounces (435 million grams) of gold. Both mines, however, are deep and old, meaning the company is experiencing increasing difficulty in extracting profitable amounts of gold from the reserves. Both mines now yield less than 0.4 ounces (12.4 grams) of gold per ton of ore and may need to be closed in the near future.

Progress on Dene Land Claims

The growth of the Northwest Territories' mining industry inevitably led to friction between newcomers to the area and the native peoples who had lived on the land for centuries. The disputes involved everything from land claims to

■ *An underground miner in Yellowknife's Giant Mine transports gold-bearing ore to the surface for milling.*

■ Murder at the Giant Mine

Long an economic pillar of Yellowknife, in 1992 the Giant Mine was the site of a labor conflict that ripped apart the community and caused wounds that fester to this day. Although the Giant Mine had been profitable for decades, its efficiency began to wane in the late 1980s. In 1990, Royal Oak Mines bought the struggling mine and put a cost-cutting executive in charge. In 1992, the labor agreement between company management and union workers, which controlled workers' pay and benefits, was set to expire. Royal Oaks announced it wanted to cut workers' pay. The unhappy miners planned to strike, but company executives beat the workers to the punch, locking them out of negotiations and flying in replacement workers.

As the labor conflict stretched from weeks into months, tensions between the newly hired replacement workers and the locked-out union workers erupted in fights, vandalism, and threats traded back and forth. Then, on September 18, 1992, a powerful bomb exploded beneath an underground rail car. Nine mine workers were killed in Canada's worst episode of labor violence. A union miner eventually confessed to the crime and was convicted of murder. Now in prison, he has recently said he falsely confessed in order to end the conflict. His supporters are pushing for a new trial while denying that any other miners played a role in the incident.

The aftereffects of the violent bombing have shaken the small city to its core. Even today, bitterness exists on both sides, and the community is divided in its allegiances. "The wounds left by the 18-month strike-lockout, the killings, and the fallout from one of the largest murder investigations in [Royal Canadian Mounted Police] history, have yet to heal," Jonathon Gatehouse proclaimed in a recent cover-story retrospective on the case in *Maclean's* magazine. He notes that Yellowknife residents cross town streets to avoid each other, and families of the dead have filed numerous wrongful death suits. Moreover, lawyers from the Association in Defence of the Wrongly Convicted are in Yellowknife reinvestigating the case. Gatehouse says that "the welcome they get from locals, many of whom wish the rest of the world would just forget the darkest chapter in the city's history, might be as cold as the winter wind across Great Slave Lake."

potential environmental effects. For example, in 1962 the Canadian government closed the uranium mine Labine had founded at Great Bear Lake, though not before the mine may have caused widespread health problems among miners and local residents. The Dene village of Deline has been dubbed "a village of widows" because of all the Dene men who died from cancer that locals attribute to working in the mine or being exposed to pollution it generated. In 1999, Canada signed a commitment with the Deline Dene Band to clean up an estimated 1.7 million tons of radioactive mine tailings in the vicinity of Great Bear Lake's aptly named Port Radium.

Such mining-related disputes were symptomatic of fundamental differences the Dene had with the territorial and federal governments. As a result, in the 1970s the Dene began years of negotiations that challenged the then-current interpretations of Treaties 8 and 11, signed in 1899 and 1921, respectively. The government's native affairs department describes the conflict as follows:

> For the most part, the Crown entered into the historic treaties with the intention of obtaining land surrenders from the different Aboriginal people occupying much of what is now present-day Canada. . . . The Treaty First Nations, on the other hand, entered into the historic treaties seeking to share their lands and resources in exchange for needed assistance from the Crown, which would in turn enhance their ability to pursue their traditional lifestyle and maintain their livelihood while making the transition to a new economy.[12]

While the treaties had set aside land for reserves, the Dene had never wanted reserves and had not received some lands set aside for them. Further, the Dene challenged the idea that they had surrendered their lands. The possibility of a natural gas pipeline being built down the Mackenzie River valley heightened the dispute since native peoples wanted to be included in project planning, determinations on the use of the land, and potential economic benefits. The federal government held that the treaties were valid but was willing to negotiate with the Dene on issues relating to whether the government had fulfilled its treaty obligations.

Lawsuits persisted throughout the 1980s before the government and several of the bands involved reached an agreement. Other bands hesitated to sign the agreement reached at that time, and some land claims still persist today. Terms of the agreement differ among bands, but, in general, bands were guaranteed certain lands, ownership of materials under portions of that land, and tax-free cash payments over extended periods of time. The agreements have paved the way for further development in the territory today.

Inuit Land Claims Lead to Nunavut

Proposed mining and pipeline projects also served to spur the Inuit to collectively bargain with the federal government for greater political independence. Because the Inuit had not signed any treaties, they never relinquished any claims to the land. Negotiations between the Inuit of the Mackenzie River delta area and the government culminated in 1984 with an agreement that guaranteed Inuvialuit ownership of 35,000 square miles (90,650 square kilometers) of land and subsurface rights to 5,000 square miles (12,950 square kilometers) of land. Further, the Inuvialuit won a cash payment of $45 million that was paid in annual installments until 1997; they also won resource co-management agreements, special harvesting rights, and other economic incentives.

But the biggest land claim was that of the central and eastern Inuit. They presented a claim in 1976 that surpassed all others in Canada and set off a long period of negotiations. In 1993 the Inuit reached an agreement with the government that guaranteed them ownership of 136,000 square miles (352,240 square kilometers) of land, $1.14 billion in cash to be spread out in annual payments until 2007, and clear rules on the rights and obligations toward the land, water, and resources. Further, as part of the agreement, the government recommended to the legislature that a new territory be created that would guarantee the Inuit a form of self-government. That territory came into being on April 1, 1999, and is called Nunavut.

Promise of Economic Success

The land claim agreements for both the Dene and Inuit illustrate the tensions that have long existed in the territory between native peoples and newcomers, whether settlers or mining prospectors. But the territory's diverse peoples are also a source of vitality that has shaped the territory's character and today puts the territory on the cusp of greater economic success.

Life in the Territory Today

The Northwest Territories remains largely uninhabited today. Consider that spread throughout a land bigger than California, Oregon, Washington, and Nevada combined can be found approximately the same number of people as live in the Los Angeles suburb of Beverly Hills. While some areas in the territory have grown quickly, often in response to a mineral strike, other places remain largely isolated, many providing homes for people of traditional cultures that have long dwelled on the land. "Even the region's most isolated communities," however, "have joined the modern world, relegating tipis, igloos, and dogsleds to folklore,"[13] notes a recent travel guide.

The daily lives of all these people are challenging, due to geography as well as weather. Residents face difficulties in communication and travel, for example, that people farther south can barely conceive. Even so, for many, the land and climate are vital reasons to stay.

A Small But Diverse Population

The 2001 Canadian census put the Northwest Territories' population at about thirty-seven thousand people. The residents are concentrated in two sections of the province. The Inuvik region of the Mackenzie River delta holds approximately ten thousand residents, while most of the remainder live in the southern region that includes Yellowknife, Fort Smith, and Hay River. Yellowknife, with its population of approximately seventeen thousand, is the only city. In addition

■ Going with the Flow in Deline

The small town of Deline (pronounced deh-lah-nay) is home to some 650 people, roughly 600 of them members of the North Slavey nation of the Dene. The town's North Slavey name (changed from Fort Franklin in 1993) means "where the water flows," appropriate enough given that Deline is located on Great Bear Lake near the mouth of the Great Bear River, approximately 100 miles (160 kilometers) south of the Arctic Circle. The first Europeans to visit the immediate area were probably explorers John Franklin and John Richardson during their 1825 to 1827 overland trek. French traders arrived in subsequent years, leaving French names and hints of French culture everywhere, followed by Catholic missionaries.

Town residents today embrace a mixture of modern-day technology and traditional lifestyles. Many of the North Slavey still hunt and fish for part or all of their subsistence. But the town is also wired for cable television, which includes major U.S. and Canadian channels, and the town government center has high-speed Internet service to help it conduct its affairs. Health care in Deline is limited to one medical station with two nurses. Anyone who needs emergency care is flown to Yellowknife. Dentists visit periodically.

Traveling to and from Deline can be difficult and expensive. During much of the spring, summer, and fall the town is reached mainly by flights from Norman Wells. Between January and March, an ice road on the Great Bear River allows goods to be trucked in from Yellowknife or the provinces. Most visitors come to Deline during the summer to fish on Great Bear Lake or to experience the town's traditional games, dances, and events.

Overall, like many northern towns, Deline is expensive because of the high cost of travel and shipping. Still, residents and tourists alike love the natural surroundings, and those who call it home have learned to accept its hardships.

the territory holds four towns, one village, and about two dozen hamlets, settlements, and charter communities. These range in population size from fewer than one hundred in Trout Lake to almost four thousand in Hay River.

One of the most striking features of the territory's population is how evenly it is divided along demographic lines. Roughly half the people are aboriginals, including First Nations, Inuit, and Métis. (French for "mixed," most Métis are descendants of French fur traders who married Indian women.) The nonnative population is dominated by young people in their twenties and thirties, many of whom are drawn to the territory by high-paying jobs and the opportunities for outdoor recreation. The nonnative population is somewhat transient, as older people tend to leave for more comfortable situations elsewhere. One estimate is that over a ten-year period, the entire nonnative population of the city of Yellowknife turns over completely. The diverse and ever-changing character of the territory gives it a unique balance and tension when compared with the provinces and other territories of Canada.

For the most part, territory residents are cooperative and considerate with each other in their daily lives. Speaking of non-aboriginal concerns in a recent interview, Northwest Territories premier Stephen Kakfwi praised the territory's diversity and welcoming attitude:

> The non-Aboriginal population want a home. They want to feel like they are part of a family. They want to have a sense that their values and traditions will be respected. This is one of the most welcoming places in Canada, and I think that can continue in large part.[14]

Because there are so few people and so many challenges from living in the north, residents often turn to the government for employment and social programs to maintain their ways of life.

Government by Consensus

The territorial government is unique in Canada, due to both its structure and its ethnic makeup. Its basic organization is similar to that of provincial governments. The territory is divided into nineteen political districts, seven of which cover parts of Yellowknife, plus others like Mackenzie Delta and North Slave. Residents of each district elect a legislator, all of whom run as independents, to represent them for a four-year term in the Legislative Assembly. The assembly selects from among its members a premier (the selection process is held as a public forum), a speaker, and an executive cabinet to include the premier and six others. The territorial government must make decisions in consultation with the federal government, which is represented by a commissioner appointed in Ottawa.

What is unusual about the structure of local government in the Northwest Territories is the absence of political parties. Politicians attempt to rule by compromise and consensus. "The consensus system of governing is more in keeping with

■ *The fourteenth Leg-islative Assembly of the Northwest Territories.*

the way that aboriginal peoples have traditionally made deci-sions," according to the Legislative Assembly website. "Unanimous agreement is not necessary for decisions to be made, motions passed, and legislation enacted. A simple majority carries the vote."[15] In practice, the legislators who are not on the executive cabinet act much like an opposition party.

The legislature, like the overall population, is about half na-tive and half nonnative. In 2002, the government was led by a native, Premier Kakfwi, who is a Sahtu (Great Bear Lake) leg-islative member and former head of the Dene Nation. Women are somewhat underrepresented in the 14th Legislative Assem-bly, however, holding only two of the nineteen seats.

The result of this non-adversarial structure and ethnic di-versity is a government that emphasizes native and nonnative cooperation in schooling, community activities, and employ-ment. The government is also aggressive in representing na-tive concerns and land claims to the federal government. Yet the government is not immune to the types of ethical issues that arise in political systems around the world. In 2002, for example, the executive cabinet briefly became embroiled in a public scandal that involved charges of conflicts of interest and secret taping of telephone calls. "The flaw in consensus government," noted *Inuvik Drum* columnist Terry Halifax, "is that there is no official opposition to act as watchdog." He goes on to say:

> Other than sporadic bursts of discontent fired from individual members, there is no organized review of the government's actions. With each member scrambling to fulfill their mandate . . . and work on committees, there is no time for eternal vigilance. . . . This form of government fosters mismanagement and breeds corruption, because it has no restraint or accountability.[16]

The territorial government recognizes the potential for abuse and has taken steps to ensure ethical behavior among legislators. For example, a 1999 law established a Conflict of Interest Commissioner, an officer of the Legislative Assembly who is independent from the government. Commissioners have since filed regular annual reports and followed up on charges brought by members of the public and government officials.

A Land of Many Languages

Residents of the Northwest Territories speak a variety of languages and dialects including English, French, and Inuit- and Athapaskan-based tongues. In Yellowknife, almost 90 percent of the residents speak English in their homes. In contrast, in tiny Nahanni Butte in the southwestern corner of the territory, about three-quarters of the eighty residents claim South Slavey as their mother tongue, with the remainder claiming English. In Inuvik, nearly all of the three thousand residents speak English fluently, but the Inuit language Inuvialuktun is the mother tongue of almost two hundred people. Others speak French, as well, a testament in part to the heritage of the traders and peoples that met during the last century.

■ *Stephen Kakfwi headed the Northwest Territories' Dene Nation and served in the Legislative Assembly for thirteen years before being elected premier in 2000.*

■ Listening to the Language Czar

A dramatic example of multiculturalism in the Northwest Territories is its official recognition not only of French and English but of nine additional aboriginal languages as well. Passed in 1984, the territory's Official Languages Act, modeled on a federal act of the same name, guaranteed equal status for English and French in government services and programs, including health boards and courts but not municipal governments or private businesses. The act also made the government of the Northwest Territories the first body in Canada to officially recognize the aboriginal languages in use at the time. The law has since been amended to include the following aboriginal languages: Chipewyan, Cree, Dogrib, Gwich'in, North Slavey, South Slavey, and the three Inuit languages of Inuktitut, Inuinnaqtun, and Inuvialuktun. This means that residents can use any of these eleven official languages to communicate with or receive services from departments, boards, and agencies of the territorial government. The Canada-NWT Cooperation Agreement on Languages also mandates that translation services be provided in the official languages to school students needing such services.

The Northwest Territories government has also established an official Languages Commissioner to make sure that the spirit of the act pervades the territory. "Our languages are so important," Languages Commissioner Fibbie Tatti, a Dene from Deline, said in 2001. "People need to work together if our languages are to survive." The territorial government contends that aboriginal languages will slowly die out if not given official support. It notes that a recent two-year review of the federal Official Languages Act determined that the use of aboriginal languages had declined despite a federal investment of $38 million over the past decade.

The territory's cultural diversity is also reflected in the numerous ways people live and survive in the far north. While Yellowknife is large enough to have three newspapers, three radio stations, and a nineteen-story skyscraper, and enjoys access to high-quality goods and services throughout the year, some tiny outposts of population may have a single small store and only distant or intermittent services. Hamlets like Sachs Harbour and Holman in the Arctic's Amundsen Gulf, for example, can be reached only by boat or plane. Even this access is limited. The main carriers flying into Holman, for example, leave only from Inuvik and Yellowknife. Seasonal sea ice closes in on Sachs Harbour and Holman during the fall, so barges and supply ships serve the towns only during the brief summer. Many residents take the opportunity then to stock up for the year on bulk food items. For much of the rest of the year, access to mainstream consumer goods and health care is limited. Further, communication can be difficult for these tiny, far-off settlements because of atmospheric interference tied to the northern lights.

Creating Economic Diversity

Another lifestyle challenge residents of the Northwest Territories face is the general lack of diversity in employment opportunities. Provinces like Alberta and British Columbia have utilized their oil, timber, and other natural resources to attract jobs. Royalties from the sale of these resources have also helped provinces build their infrastructure, including the transportation and communications industries. As a result Vancouver, Edmonton, and Calgary have developed into centers for high-tech industry, health care, and education. Energy and mineral exploitation has become the main economic engine of the Northwest Territories as well, though the difficulties in developing transportation and communication networks are much greater. Thus, government and tourism take on extra importance.

Like overall employment, job diversity differs from region to region, town to town. In Yellowknife, the most important employer by far is the government of the Northwest Territories, followed by the federal government. Along with local school boards and the city of Yellowknife, they employ about one-third of the eleven-thousand-person workforce. The regional hospital, Miramar Mining, and BHP Billiton Diamonds are the next-largest employers. Many other Yellowknife residents work in finance, utility, or tourist oriented industries. City officials say that the near future may bring more jobs in the oil and natural gas industry.

In stark contrast to Yellowknife is tiny Rae Lakes, located at the end of a winter ice road some 150 miles (240 kilometers) northwest of Yellowknife. Rae Lakes' population is slightly less than 300 people, nearly all of whom are aboriginal (Dogrib). More than a third of the labor force participate in traditional jobs such as hunting, trapping, and fishing. The

■ A Failed Pipeline Becomes a Tourist Attraction

One of the more unusual wilderness attractions in the Northwest Territories is a trail that follows the former service road of an abandoned, World War II-era oil pipeline. The so-called Canol (short for "Canadian oil") Heritage Trail, which starts across the Mackenzie River from Norman Wells, runs for 200 miles (350 kilometers) through the rugged Mackenzie Mountains to the border with Yukon Territory. From there a road has been built to White-horse, Yukon's capital city.

The Canol pipeline was conceived during the early 1940s when Canada and the United States were jointly building a much bigger project, the Alaska Highway that now connects Dawson Creek in British Columbia with Fairbanks, Alaska. U.S. politicians were worried that the country's west coast oil reserves might be threatened by Japanese strikes. An alternative, Canadian source of fuel could come from oil fields near Norman Wells, with a pipeline transporting crude oil more than six hundred miles (one thousand kilometers) to a refinery in Whitehorse. Between 1942 and 1944, twenty-five thousand Canadian and American workers faced terrible conditions and difficult technical obstacles to construct the pipeline. The project ultimately cost the U.S. government more than $100 million. Unfortunately, the relatively small amounts of oil the pipeline could transport (the small-diameter tubing used was obsolete even at the start of the project) were not needed—the threat to west coast oil supplies was overstated—by the time the pipeline opened in February 1944. The pipeline functioned (and malfunctioned—the effects of oil spills remain visible today) for a year or so before officials shut it down. While some of the machinery was sal-

government and school are major employers, accounting for roughly 40 percent of those employed. Nearly all others work in the mining industry or in the local community hall, store, or airstrip.

In a number of towns in the far north, such as Tuktoyaktuk, Sachs Harbour, and Holman, much of the small population is Inuit. Some of the residents hold government or teaching jobs, or work in the service or oil industries, while others participate in hunting, trapping, and fishing. Tourism, outfitting, and arts and crafts are also popular. In Holman, printmaking employs a significant sector of the economy.

vaged, equipment and vehicles were abandoned, and large portions of the pipeline remain intact today.

The route of the Canol pipeline's service road in the Northwest Territories now serves as a challenging wilderness trail trekked and (in some parts) mountain-biked mainly from mid-July to early September. Because the trail is not actively maintained, however, and it is one of the most remote trails in Canada, it attracts mainly the most dedicated and experienced adventurers. Hiking its length takes three weeks and requires difficult river crossings, protecting food from bears, and dealing with swarms of mosquitoes. Those who are willing to make the endeavor can experience a unique view of natural and human-made history.

■ *Mountain biking along the Canol Heritage Trail is a challenging but rewarding wilderness experience.*

Facing the High Cost of Living

Residents of the Northwest Territories earn, on average, more money than do other Canadians. In 2001, the average income among all wage-earning people in the territory was almost $34,000, which is substantially higher than the national average of just under $30,000. But territorial residents also pay far more for goods and services than do people "south of sixty." Further, wide variations among living standards exist from place to place, in large part because of variations in the unemployment rate.

The high cost of living is the main reason that the higher earnings do not necessarily translate to better standards of living. This is particularly true in the dozen or so exceptionally remote hamlets that do not have four-season (or any) roads, all of which face the sky-high costs associated with flying in all goods. For example, a roundtrip airline ticket from Holman to Yellowknife may cost more than $1,500. Because Holman has only one business that sells gasoline and heating oil, residents can hardly be choosy about the price they pay for these goods. Only two local merchants sell clothing and hardware, though residents can also rely on the barge shipments they receive in the summertime for some goods. Food prices are approximately twice as high in Holman and Sachs Harbour as they are in Yellowknife, where prices are already lofty by Canadian standards.

Compared to fly-in communities, the cost of goods and services in the territory's other towns and hamlets is somewhat lower. Even so, residents often face high payments to cover the basics of food, housing, fuel for transportation and home heating, and even entertainment. Shipping costs remain a prime culprit. The lack of commercial agriculture, for example, means that almost all of the territory's fruits, vegetables, grains, and other produce must be shipped in from Saskatchewan, Ontario, and elsewhere. The same goes for major appliances—a television set that costs about $600 in much of Canada will generally run $1,000 or more in Yellowknife. The lack of transportation infrastructure is another factor. No bridges cross the Liard or Mackenzie rivers (ferries operate in a number of places) and winter ice roads and bridges need to be reestablished every year. The territorial government recently backed down from a proposal to finance highway upgrades with a trip permit fee on commercial trucking due to protests over the fee's potential to increase the cost of living.

In 2002 the territorial government reached an agreement with a private corporation, the Fort Providence Combined Council Alliance, to build a two-lane, half-mile-(one-kilometer) long bridge across the Mackenzie River at Fort Providence. Commercial traffic would pay a toll, but trucking companies have welcomed the proposed bridge since they currently pay about $500 per day when a truck has to wait for the ferry or the ice road to operate. The bridge may open to traffic as early as 2005.

Education: Where High-Tech and Heritage Mix

Establishing a top-notch educational system in the territory is a major goal for the territorial government. Studies show that territory residents who have less than a ninth grade education earn about $14,000 per year; a high school diploma brings average earnings to $18,000 per year; trade school or other university training yields an average of more than $30,000 per year; and those achieving university diplomas average more than $50,000 per year. With these statistics in mind, the government has set out to improve education for all children and adults in the territory, while preserving and honoring the heritage of the many cultures.

Currently, the Northwest Territories has some fifty elementary and high schools, including three private schools and two Francophone (French-speaking) schools, serving a total of approximately ten thousand students. The system is run by the territorial Department of Education, seven regional boards of education, and local administrators. The territorial government has determined that schools should emphasize core subjects as well as aboriginal culture, heritage, and language. The government has also recently been pushing technology to the forefront of education.

Relatively high levels of government funding for education in recent years have helped to raise average education levels in the territory. In fact, the Northwest Territories is one of the few Canadian jurisdictions that saw substantial increases in high school graduation rates from 1996 to 2001. Increasing numbers of territorial students are also going on to either trade school or university.

Yellowknife's Catholic School District offers the only religious educational option within the territory. As is true in a number of provinces, the Northwest Territories helps to fund religious education, in this case providing about 70 percent of the revenue for the Catholic School District's general operations. Close to fifteen hundred students attend three Catholic schools. One is a K–8 English school while the other two (a K–8 and a high school) are both dual-track French and English immersion schools. The Catholic schools are ethnically mixed—35 percent of those attending the Catholic high school are aboriginal—and focus on cultural heritage issues as well as religious beliefs.

■ A Visit to Two Territorial Schools

Schools in the main urban setting of Yellowknife rival many of the better schools of any province. For example, Range Lake North elementary (K–8) school in Yellowknife opened in 1993 and has since developed a number of innovative programs in the areas of student leadership and technology integration. In addition to gaining a greater respect for cultures and the environment, Range Lake North students can learn basic keyboarding skills or take more advanced topics in computers and electronics. The school's computer lab and classrooms house an impressive array of high-tech equipment that includes dozens of late-model Macintosh desktop and portable computers, scanners, laser printers, and digital cameras. All of the school's computers are Ethernet-networked and connected to the Internet.

Remote communities face greater challenges in providing a broad and rich range of educational opportunities. For example, Helen Kalvak School, the only school in Holman, until 2002 offered courses only through grade eleven. Instruction is in English, though one of the school's ten teachers also instructs students in the traditional language of the community, Inuinnaqtun. Like many schools in larger communities, though, Helen Kalvak School is Internet accessible, and its curriculum includes a strong focus on science and technology.

■ *Students at Yellowknife's Range Lake North elementary school have access to top-notch computer technology.*

The only college in the Northwest Territories is publicly funded Aurora College, which has campuses in Fort Smith, Yellowknife, and Inuvik. Its programs range from basic adult education to diamond cutting and polishing to management studies. Students can obtain trade certificates or university credits toward a degree. Further, the college supports the Aurora Research Institute at Inuvik, whose mandate is to use scientific, technological, and aboriginal knowledge to address the problems unique to the north, such as the effect of forest fires and climate change on northern communities.

■ *Researchers from the Aurora Research Institute study invertebrate samples in the field.*

A Growing Cultural Awareness

The Northwest Territories is a society in transition. Its strength is in the diversity and determination of its people, all of whom share a willingness to brave difficult conditions and a commitment to multicultural understanding. Initiatives to create new jobs and to improve education and training have improved the lives of both natives and nonnatives in recent years. The emphasis on cultural awareness in education has created a greater spirit of cooperation among the territory's residents. The weather can be oppressive and the land uncompromising, but for those who enjoy these challenges, their lives are rewarding.

Arts and Culture

CHAPTER

5

T hough small in population, the Northwest Territories is diverse in artistic and cultural expression. With so many backgrounds to draw from, residents of the territory readily exhibit their traditions in dancing, theater, and art. Virtually every town and village relies on such expressions to create jobs and, perhaps more important, to celebrate and pass on their heritage. From multi-day celebrations in Yellowknife to the smallest town festivals, from modern theater to traditional games, the residents of the territory offer a range of artistic and cultural attractions. In addition, many of those who live in the territory love the outdoors— the rugged mountains, the mighty rivers and lakes, the almost untouched forests and hills. With territory so large, there is both much to celebrate and much to explore.

Yellowknife: A Cultural Crossroads

Because the bulk of the territory's population resides in Yellowknife, a great number of the territory's artistic offerings can be found here as well. The city serves as a cultural crossroads that features folk festivals, native dance troupes, celebrations of the early European explorers and mountaineers, dogsled races, and more. Many celebrations highlight the heritage and traditions of the past, while others welcome local artists and musicians as well as international performers who give residents of the territory a taste of the latest trends from the south.

Each year in July, Yellowknife hosts the three-day Folk on the Rocks music festival, a relatively new attraction that draws acts not only from within the territory but also from elsewhere in Canada, the United States, and abroad. In recent years, the territorial acts have included those rooted in native traditions

69

■ *Yellowknife's annual Folk on the Rocks music festival attracts performers from the territory as well as from Nunavut, Alaska, and "the South."*

as well as those on the forefront of performance art, from world music to slam poetry. For example, Aqsarniit (ak-sar-nee), an Inuit group from Nunavut, invents new dances and music based upon traditional Inuit melodies and movements. A stark contrast in a recent festival was Mother Divine, a hard-rock group from Inuvik that relied on thunderous guitar play to shake the audience. Visitors to the festival, held on the shores of Long Lake outside Yellowknife, enjoy music and performances, food, and workshops with their favorite performers.

Before the summer Folk on the Rocks festival, the spring-time Caribou Carnival is a culturally uniting festival for the territory. The annual week-long March celebration features modern and traditional games, community activities, and skill contests that recall the days of the early native peoples and the first European explorers. Competitions include log sawing, spike driving, snowshoe racing, pillow fighting, and igloo building. Dene tribes put on demonstrations, and male and female challengers compete for the titles of King and Queen of the carnival. Adventurous eaters at the event can try char chowder, caribou burgers, and dried musk ox. The city of Yellowknife officially observes a half-day civic holiday on the Friday of every Caribou Carnival week.

No winter in Yellowknife is complete without its annual Dog Derby. When it first started in 1955, the dogsled race featured thirteen contestants, a forty-mile (sixty-five-kilometer) course, and prizes of $50 for the winner and sacks of flour and groceries for runner-ups. The end-of-March race now draws corporate sponsorship and international contestants, covers 150 miles (240 kilometers) broken into three 50-mile (80-

kilometer) heats, and awards more than $35,000 in prizes, including a $10,000 top prize. The dog teams are made up of four to ten dogs pulling a driver on a racing sled or toboggan. A recent addition to the festivities is the Heritage Race in which dogsled contestants race a short loop that includes a stop where they must boil water and make tea.

Art and Theater in the City

In addition to the cultural celebrations and competitions, Yellowknife hosts some of the territory's strongest theatrical and artistic offerings. Like the festivals, art and theater in the city mingle the traditional with the modern.

The city's theater is a prime example of the creative mixture of traditional knowledge and modern storytelling. Stuck in a Snowbank Theatre, the only professional theater company in the Northwest Territories, delights audiences throughout the territory and across Canada with tales of the north that are written, produced, and performed by northerners. It specializes in converting oral traditions and historical writings into dynamic theatrical performances. The theater's offerings have been home-grown and diverse: *Ingilraat Pitquhivut Tammanagit* (Before Our Traditional Ways Disappear) was a collaboration between the theater and the Elders Centre in Kugluktuk, Nunavut. The theater's director and choreographer used hundreds of translated pages of oral

■ *Dogsled racing is a winter sport of the north that makes use of traditional survival and endurance skills.*

■ *Stuck in a Snowbank Theatre's production of* The Arctic Circle War *offered new insights into the character of Albert "Mad Trapper" Johnson.*

history to create a community theater piece that was performed using only the elders and the youth of the community. Stuck in a Snowbank Theatre has also produced a highly acclaimed play based on the chilling story of the Mad Trapper, the hermit who killed a Mountie and then eluded authorities for over a month during a winter wilderness chase in the early 1930s. Further, the theater has collaborated with community organizations, such as the Centre for Community Living, to produce works that promote tolerance and unity.

The Prince of Wales Northern Heritage Centre in Yellowknife holds a vast repository of Northwest Territories' history. The architecturally impressive center, located on the shores of Frame Lake, includes a museum and the territory's official archives. Its artifacts, artworks, and historical exhibits preserve the rich cultural heritage of the territory. The center's holdings represent ancient native cultures as well as the earliest European explorers. The center posts online exhibits to allow viewers to learn about history and the center's many items. Interested web surfers can find articles on the Dogrib Tea Dance, research Franklin's tragic fate, or play the Deh Cho Board Game. Prince of Wales also offers heritage programs that extend beyond the walls of the center.

Small Town Traditions

While Yellowknife is the hub of artistic and cultural activities in the territory, many of the territory's small towns and hamlets have their own traditions and cultural expressions. These range from simple, day-to-day recreational activities to festivals and gatherings that attract thousands from around the territory. In tiny Fort Liard, a hamlet near the border of British Columbia, fur traders still come to trade their goods and buy supplies for life in the wilderness. The area, dominated by the Kaska and Acho Dene, is connected daily to its heritage and culture through activities, products, and architecture.

■ The Mysterious Mad Trapper of the North

Just after Christmas in 1931, four officers of the Royal Canadian Mounted Police and a civilian made their way into the wilderness near Fort McPherson. They knocked at the tiny cabin of Albert Johnson, a newcomer to the area who was reportedly trapping without a license. They were answered by a gunshot that hit the lead officer in the chest, gravely wounding him. The party retreated to Aklavik but soon returned with reinforcements.

What followed was dubbed the "Arctic Circle War" by the press, though as wars go it was a relatively benign one, with only two fatalities. Johnson led some one hundred Mounties and their native guides on a five-week chase through the wilds of the Northwest Territories and the Yukon, apparently heading for Alaska. The wilderness man with a mysterious past masterfully eluded his trackers, keeping to wind-swept trails that made him nearly untraceable. "Albert Johnson seemed to be no average trapper," according to "Mysteries of Canada" writer Jack Harley. "The Mounties said of him to be capable of great feats and crafty beyond belief. The local Inuit said at one point in the chase that Johnson could snowshoe 2 miles for every 1 mile a dog team had to break trail."

Only twice did the Mounties encounter him. The first time resulted in a gun battle during which Johnson killed one officer and pinned down the others. The second encounter, with a tracking airplane overhead, left one officer wounded and Johnson bleeding from nine gunshot wounds. Johnson died without revealing anything about himself, and no family members ever identified him. Authorities found on him $2,000 in cash and some gold.

Theories have abounded about the Mad Trapper for years. Some think he was a Chicago gangster on the run from the law, while others say that he was searching for a gold mine rumored to be in the area.

■ Urban Indian Leela Gilday

One of the Northwest Territories' most popular musical artists is Leela Gilday, a Dene who brings what she calls "an urban Indian sensibility" to her singing and songwriting. Gilday began singing professionally as a preteen in Yellowknife during the early 1980s and went on to receive classical voice training at the University of Alberta. She blends moods and mixes blues, jazz, and other styles in her music, much of which addresses her love of the North. Her work has attracted attention throughout the territory, where she co-hosted the 1999 Folk on the Rocks music festival, and across the nation. She appeared at the 1998 National Aboriginal Achievement Awards and in 2000 hosted a CBC broadcast on the spiritual nature of Easter called "God's Own Juke Box." Further, she has appeared on television specials and has performed at many venues in the north and across the country. She is an outspoken advocate of aboriginal rights, and she carries her message in song and speech wherever she goes. With so much passion and plenty of years ahead, Gilday remains an important northern artist to watch.

■ *Singer and songwriter Leela Gilday draws upon her Dene roots and a classically-trained voice to explore various themes.*

Shoppers can choose among such popular traditional items as birchbark baskets and handcrafted moose hide moccasins. One of the finest buildings to visit in the hamlet is a Catholic church built by Oblate missionaries with hand-sawn lumber between 1913 and 1921. Catholicism in the hamlet dates to the 1860s, and the church building is still used for services. Beyond that, Fort Liard hosts a small boat tour service that takes residents and tourists on the Liard River. A knowledgeable guide informs travelers about the area and its heritage while leading one-hour, half-day, or even full-day trips.

The larger Great Slave Lake town of Hay River offers a cultural scene that is more diverse than Fort Liard's. The year's big event is Heritage Days, held in early June as the summer fisheries open. The three-day event opens with a parade and a half-day holiday for town residents. Subsequent days include a pancake breakfast, a soapbox derby for kids, an Ethnic Food Fest, and a raft race in which competitors must first build their rafts from supplied logs. The town also becomes reflective on the second day during the Blessing of the Fleet and the Laying of the Wreath ceremonies, events that honor those who have died on Great Slave Lake and ask for good fortune to those venturing out in the coming season. Heritage Days wraps up on the third day with a hearty fish fry.

The Dene Cultural Institute, which was established in 1987 in the basement of a Yellowknife office building, moved its operations to the Hay River Dene Reserve in 1991. Now known as the Yamozha Kue, the institute is widely respected for its work in protecting and promoting the language and culture of the Dene. It has recently expanded into a graceful log-and-stone building that was designed with the help of Dene elders. The Dene plan an extended array of arts and crafts workshops, multimedia presentations, theater performances, display exhibits, and other cultural demonstrations in the spacious structure. The institute is also working on a website to share the Dene heritage with interested people around the world.

■ *Drumming plays an important part in Dene healing and celebrations. Dene drums like those being used here were traditionally made from moose or caribou skin stretched over a wood frame and sewn with sinew.*

■ The Great Norman Wells Fossil Hunt

The Mackenzie River town of Norman Wells is home to one of the most unique town events in the territory: an annual fossil hunt that takes place over eight days in early August. The event attracts paleontologists as well as amateurs eager for their first find.

Norman Wells just happens to sit atop a fabulous repository of fossils, and residents and visitors alike find fossils all over the town and surrounding areas. Every year, new discoveries are made on the banks of the river, beside the roads in town, or in the surrounding hills, valleys, and canyons. Nearby, a ridge of 400-million-year-old Devonian limestone and shale yields corals, sponges, and shells. Elsewhere, residents can find fossilized trilobites (an extinct marine invertebrate), petrified wood and amber, and even unnamed fossils that have yet to be classified. The event draws not only fossil hunters but also rock collectors in search of pyrite ("fool's gold") nodules, calcite crystals, and other unique rocks and minerals. The fossil festival includes crafts and activities for children, community barbecues, canoe trips on Jackfish Lake, and hikes into Fossil Canyon.

Cultural Capital of the North

The Mackenzie delta town of Inuvik is a key cultural center throughout the far north. Since it is about 60 percent non-aboriginal, 25 percent Inuvialuit, and 15 percent Dene, Inuvik mixes elements of the territory's three main cultures. It hosts portions of the annual Arctic Winter Games Territorial Trials (in 2002, the Inuvik events were dog mushing, hockey, and soccer), and it is home to celebrations like the Sunrise Festival in January and the Delta Daze festival in November. One of the territory's most distinctive buildings is Inuvik's igloo-shaped Church of Our Lady of Victory.

Inuvik is also the site of the territory's largest and arguably its most exciting artistic festival—the Great Northern Arts Festival. The annual July festival takes place over ten days and attracts more than one hundred artists and performers from diverse cultures, including Inuvialuit, Gwich'in, Dene, and Métis. The Festival Gallery contains up to fifteen hundred pieces of art and handiwork for exhibition and sale. Past artists from the Northwest Territories have included carver Putuguk Ashevak from Taloyoak (now Nunavut), a hunter with a family of four; Mark Bleakney, a stained glass artist and full-time pharmacist in Inuvik; and Vicki Boudreau of Inuvik, a specialist in digital photography who captures haunting images of the Mackenzie River delta and the Beaufort Sea in her work. Entertainment for the festival generally includes music and storytelling. Workshops on polymer clay molding, willow basketry, soapstone carving, and other crafts offer festival-goers a chance to work closely with their favorite artists.

While artistic expressions are deeply ingrained in the territory's people, perhaps nothing is as dear to residents as the area's raw outdoor wilderness. Virtually every town and hamlet boasts of its proximity to natural wonders. Population centers rely on tourism, and most have outfitting and guiding groups that prepare tourists and residents alike for wilderness adventures of various difficulties. The residents themselves eagerly embrace their outdoor recreation, with just cause—there are nearly limitless areas of natural splendor to enjoy.

Dempster Driving

One of the best ways to get into the territory's wilderness is via a remarkable human-made feature, the Dempster Highway. This 450-mile (700-kilometer), almost-year-round gravel road connects Inuvik to Dawson City, Yukon. Since its completion in 1978 the Dempster has served as a crucial land connection for Inuvik with points south, as no road exists down the Mackenzie River valley to Fort Simpson. The Dempster closes temporarily during November and April most years, when the Peel and Mackenzie rivers, which the Dempster crosses, freeze and thaw. (No bridges ford these rivers. Ferries transport cars during the summer, whereas during the winter the rivers freeze hard enough to allow cars to simply drive across.)

The Dempster's construction and arctic location posed a number of difficult engineering challenges, a guide book notes:

> Normal road grading is impossible; if the tundra surface of permafrost is disturbed, the underlying ice begins to melt; over a period of years a marshy sinkhole develops, eventually drowning the road. Much of the Dempster is highly elevated above the tundra, in order that the warm roadbed (during periods of 24-hour sunlight, the exposed soil can absorb a lot of heat) doesn't begin to melt the permafrost.[17]

The natural wonders on display along the Dempster change with the seasons. The highway runs through two mountain ranges (the Mackenzies and the Yukon's Richardson Mountains), crosses the continental divide, and weaves back and forth across the northern limit of wooded country.

It is one of the few roads in the world that extends north of the Arctic Circle. During the winter only, the highway continues past Inuvik as an ice road to the Beaufort Sea.

Many intrepid travelers drive their cars and recreational vehicles north along the Dempster from Dawson City during the summer. The nearly twenty-four hours of daylight provide excellent viewing of the mountains and scenery. Further, those interested can stop and hike north of the tree line. Travelers coming in September and October are more likely to get glimpses of wildlife, including members of the huge Porcupine Caribou Herd (named after the Porcupine River that flows from northern Yukon Territory into Alaska) crossing the highway on their way to their winter ranges. But even hardy winter travelers enjoy spectacular sights—the many clear nights from February through April offer great views of the northern lights.

Watching for Waterfalls

■ *The Kakisa River thunders over the fifty-foot- (fifteen-meter) high Lady Evelyn Falls along the territory's picturesque "Waterfalls Route."*

Perhaps the most scenic roadway in the territory is the "Waterfalls Route" along Highway 1 in the southern part of the territories. Highway 1 extends from Fort Simpson east along the Mackenzie River to Hay River, on the southern shores of Great Slave

■ Myth and Adventure in Nahanni National Park

Located in the southwest corner of the territory and taking in the South Nahanni River and a portion of the Mackenzie Mountains, Nahanni National Park is a natural wonder and a haven of pristine wilderness. No roads enter the park—it can be reached only by walking, boating, or flying in. A number of tours operate out of Fort Simpson; even so, fewer than one thousand people visit Nahanni every year. Sections of the South Nahanni River provide world-class rapids to skilled canoeists and white-water rafters. Near Sunblood Mountain signs on the river warn of the approach of Virginia Falls, a roaring waterfall that, at roughly three hundred feet (one hundred meters), is almost twice the height of Niagara. In addition to the spectacular river canyons and falls, hikers can also find hotsprings, caves, and untouched forests of aspen and birch.

Nahanni is a native name that translates as "powerful river." Many of the park's features were named during the first decades of the twentieth century, when ill-prepared adventurers were drawn by rumors of gold. The park's Deadmen Valley, for example, was named after Willie and Frank McLeod, brothers who in 1905 went in search of a lost gold mine in the mountains. Their skeletons were

■ *Hikers in Nahanni National Park, with a massive, snow-covered mountain in the background, plan their route through the wilderness*

found three years later, huddled together. Locals speculated that a third member of their party had murdered them after the three had found gold. A year later, the remains of another body were discovered nearby. Park rangers say that, rather than foul play, it is more likely that all three men starved after losing their boat and being unable to survive the winter. "As tales of the South Nahanni spread," noted *National Geographic* writer Douglas Chadwick, "exotic vegetation and queer beasts were added to its hot springs, more and more heads were separated from the bodies of its casualties, and gold glimmered bright on its gravel bars. The country ended up with a legendary reputation and a sinister set of names: Broken Skull river, the Funeral Range, Deadmen Valley, the Headless Range, Hells Gate."

Lake, and then south into northern Alberta. Travelers along the route pass numerous parks, many with spectacular waterfalls that formed from glacial runoff at the end of the last ice age. Some of the falls are small, like the fifty-foot (seventeen-meter) falls in McNallie Creek Picnic Area. Even these offer natural splendor—creek swallows nest in the walls of the ravine that the water falls into. Other parks have much grander falls. For example, Twin Falls Territorial Park northwest of Hay River has two large waterfalls and one smaller waterfall with trails and services for easy viewing. Lady Evelyn Falls, on the Kakisa River near where the Great Slave Lake flows into the Mackenzie River, is a magnificent curtain of water tumbling over a limestone sill. Visitors can picnic and fish at the base of the waterfall.

In general, most visitors venture into the parks only during the summer, but each season offers its own striking view of the falls. In the autumn, the warm river water cascading through the cold air causes clouds of vapor to rise off the rivers. In winter, the falls are startling in their frozen grandeur, and in spring, huge chunks of melting ice tumble onto each other. All along the route, travelers can stop to camp or just to pause in places such as Kakisa or Enterprise where they can learn more about the rich culture and past of the territory.

In addition to these two routes and their attendant parks, the southern "Deh Cho Travel Connection" portion of the territory is a haven for campers, hikers, canoeists, and whitewater rafters. About halfway between Fort Liard and Fort Simpson, Blackstone Territorial Park, with its campgrounds, showers, and a visitors' center, offers outdoor enthusiasts a jumping-off point for wilderness adventures in nearby Nahanni.

Bridging the Gap

The people of the Northwest Territories are bound together and strengthened by their artistic, cultural, and recreational pursuits. While visitors may not find the sophisticated symphony and ballet companies common in the provinces to the south, they will find celebrations and traditions alive and well and plenty of outdoor activities to satisfy any recreational appetite. Further, the territory offers dynamic, innovative artistic offerings that balance the native and non-aboriginal cultures perhaps better than anywhere else in Canada. This tradition of honoring other cultures bridges the gaps between the diverse communities and provides the groundwork needed to meet the territory's many challenges ahead.

CHAPTER 6

A Territory in Transition

I n many ways, the Northwest Territories seems on the brink of a heyday. Diamonds have been found, a gas pipeline is in the works, aboriginal groups are increasingly self-governed, and the economy appears to be on an upswing. But the positive developments bring inherent challenges, as well. In 1999 the long-planned establishment of Nunavut was completed, drastically altering the physical, cultural, and political makeup of the territory. Further, the proposed gas pipeline through the Mackenzie River valley raises difficult logistical and environmental problems. Meanwhile, the tiny population and tax base presents a constant challenge to the territorial government as it tries to raise enough money to keep up basic services and overcome problems such as lack of accessibility to health care services. Yet there is an air of excitement, as the territory's residents seem to relish tackling these challenges.

Making the Transition

The creation of the new territory of Nunavut posed a number of political and administrative challenges. Federal and Northwest Territories officials worked for several years before the split to ensure a smooth transition. Government districts needed to be redrawn, and the entire public sector, from health care to schooling, had to be reworked under new institutions.

The division also raised important economic considerations for the Northwest Territories, since the loss of land shrank the population and resource base. "In the territories, population means money," notes *Northern News Service* reporter Thorunn Howatt. "The head count plays a key role when the federal government calculates transfer payments."[18] (The federal government makes annual transfer payments from the richer provinces and territories to the poorer ones to help equalize social spending throughout the nation.)

At roughly the same time Nunavut was being split off, the economy of the Northwest Territories suffered from a downturn in gold mining. Some high-income earners moved out of the territory, further weakening the tax base. The early difficulties were somewhat alleviated by a $60 million payment from the federal government to help cover the costs of the transition.

A Clarity of Purpose

With the transition now completed, the Northwest Territories finds itself in a new and exciting position. Premier Kakfwi believes the territorial split has been positive for the territory as a whole. In a fall 2002 interview, he pointed out simple logistical reasons for his belief, as well as some of the possibilities he sees:

> [The split] makes it much easier to govern. The territory is a lot smaller. . . . I think things are better. There's a tremendous sense of confidence, of determination, a clarity of purpose. In our lifetime we've gone from a hunting, trapping people to changing the Constitution of Canada, defining the rights and the role of Aboriginal people in Canada, introducing ourselves into the economy and the business community. Now, we deal with some of the largest companies in the world. Some of our people own airlines, trucking companies, real estate.[19]

The Northwest Territories lost both land area and population when Nunavut was created, but it also jettisoned a few troublesome social issues. For example, as vast as the Northwest Territories is, it has more concentrated population centers compared to Nunavut, allowing for somewhat more efficient administration and delivery of government services. Nunavut is also grappling with the political tension caused by under-representation of native people in the government. The Northwest Territories government, on the other hand, has a balance of non-aboriginals and native peoples in elected office.

■ What's in a Name?

The five hundred residents of Fort Norman, at the confluence of the Mackenzie and Great Bear rivers, woke up on January 1, 1996, with new addresses even though they had not moved anywhere. That is because the name of their town had been officially changed to Tulita, a North Slavey name meaning "where the waters meet." Fort Norman was one of a half-dozen towns in the territory during the 1990s that saw its name changed from a European name to a native name, including Fort Franklin to Deline, Arctic Red River to Tsiigehtchic, and Lac La Martre to Wekweti. Traditional names often evoke local natural features rather than a pioneering individual, as do many European names. Thus the Inuvialuit refer to Sachs Harbour as Ikaahuk, "where you go across to," and Colville Lake is K'ahbamitue, "ptarmigan net place."

The transition from European to native names is going on nationwide and promises to continue in the Northwest Territories, where more than a dozen of the thirty-plus towns and villages are already officially known by native names. The territory must work with the Ottawa-based Canadian Permanent Committee on Geographical Names to officially change place names. After centuries of imposing European names on places already identified with names by the local native groups, "Authorities at all levels now make every effort to ensure that indigenous place names are respected as an important element in Native culture," notes geographer William C. Wonders.

Agreeing upon exactly which native name should replace a European name can result in heated debates among natives. In the Northwest Territories, this is particularly true in areas that have a history of overlapping use and occupancy by Inuvialuit, Dene, and Métis groups, such as north of Great Bear Lake. Such conflicts may also save the name of the territory itself, which some political leaders have criticized for representing merely a geographic direction in relation to Ottawa. In early 2002 the territorial Legislative Assembly decided not to pursue a new name for the Northwest Territories, with members saying that other priorities should take precedence. Among the names unofficially considered were Denendeh ("land of the Dene") and Aurora. (In an online poll in 1996, "Northwest Territories" was the overwhelming winner in a popularity contest among names for the territory; somewhat embarrassingly for the territory, "Bob" came in second.)

The Mackenzie River may also eventually succumb to name change. Many Dene already routinely refer to it, and the southern section of the territories, as Deh Cho. Commercial use of the name has spread from the Deh Cho Air airline to the *Deh Cho Drum* newspaper.

■ *An elderly resident of the Colville Lake area north of Great Bear Lake forages for wild berries.*

Show Me the Money

Finding adequate funding is the common factor in many of the territory's most challenging issues. The territorial government's capacity to raise money is limited, while demands on its services are high. In addition to the money the territorial government receives from the federal government as transfer payments, the federal government also makes a special payment to the territories in recognition of their unique challenges and the higher costs of providing public services in the north. The federal government estimated that in 2002–2003, these transfers to the Northwest Territories would total $413 million (compared to $538 million in 1999–2000), or about $10,000 per person. These payments would account for almost half of the Northwest Territories' government revenues. The bulk of this money goes into social programs, including health care services, education, and justice systems, for residents of the territory.

Most of the rest of the territorial budget comes from various taxes. But because the population is small, the personal and corporate tax base is limited. Even though workers' average wages are generally slightly higher in the Northwest Territories than elsewhere in Canada, the high cost of living offsets these gains and reduces tax revenues.

Worse for the territory, its ability to take advantage of its growing industries is limited. The federal government retains control over virtually all of the natural resources within the territory, in contrast to the power the federal government has delegated to provincial governments over the natural resources within their boundaries. Thus, taxes and royalties paid by oil, gas, and mineral corporations doing business in the Northwest Territories flow directly to the federal rather than to the territorial government. Territorial officials contend that federal transfer payments only partially offset this arrangement. Who should pay for specific projects is thus a constant battle, as Kakfwi noted:

> The highways around here are disintegrating, mostly because of the 8,000 trucks a year that roll north to supply the diamond mines. The diamond mines are paying royalties to the federal government, but the federal government has yet to produce any money to fix those roads. Right now, Canada owns all the land and the resources in the Northwest Territories. But it doesn't belong to them, it belongs to us. It belongs to the Aboriginal people and it will belong to the northern people who also make this their home.[20]

Kakfwi and other territorial officials have begun negotiations to change the revenue agreements with the federal government and update the law that covers control of resources

■ *Commercial fishermen pull in a net on the Hay River in southern Northwest Territories.*

within the territory. Leaders are optimistic and see the move as important both economically and symbolically. If the territory succeeds in evolving a new relationship with the federal government, and various resource projects (particularly the yet-to-be-built natural gas pipeline and the fast-growing diamond industry) reach their full potential, the Northwest Territories could become the nation's first territory to become economically self-sufficient.

Easing Taxes and Growing Jobs

The economic reality of the present is that the Northwest Territories must struggle to provide a decent standard of living for its residents. In the short term, territorial officials are hoping to ease the burden of the high cost of food, housing, and energy by using tax cuts to put more money in its residents' hands. In 2002 the government introduced a minimum cost of living tax credit, allowing low-income residents to pay less money in taxes. The territory increased the level of tax credits available to individuals, married couples, the elderly, and the disabled. In addition, it raised the dollar level at which low-income earners are exempt from taxes. All of these changes effectively put more than $7 million in people's hands, money that can make a big difference in many small communities.

The government is also focused on creating and attracting jobs for territorial residents, especially in the small communities where there has traditionally been little economic activity. Until very recently, even the larger towns lacked the type of economic diversity found in most locales in the provinces. As a result, in the late 1990s, unemployment in the Northwest Territories was often higher than 13 percent, well above the Canadian national average of 7 to 9 percent. It is only since the separation with Nunavut, and with the rapid growth in diamond mining in recent years, that unemployment in the Northwest Territories has fallen. By the fall of 2002, in fact, the territory's unemployment rate of 5.7 percent was the second-lowest of Canada's provinces and territories, and well below the national average of 7.7 percent.

Job growth was especially evident in Yellowknife and in the four towns (Hay River, Inuvik, Fort Smith, and Rae-Edzo) with populations in the two thousand to four thousand range. Well-paying private-sector jobs were scarcer in the small villages and hamlets of the Northwest Territories, where traditional subsistence jobs such as hunting, fishing, and trapping still persevere. Disparities continue to exist as well in employment among racial and ethnic groups. The unemployment rate among natives is often about double that of nonnatives.

Even when jobs are available in northern communities, it can sometimes be difficult to find qualified employees, from teachers to bankers, willing to relocate. In the fall of 2001, a national teacher shortage left Yellowknife schools scrounging for substitute teachers. The Mackenzie River delta area lost more than half of its teachers at the end of the 2000–2001 school year, and the local education council had difficulty filling teaching vacancies.

A Focus on Social Services

The loss of some of the territory's best-educated and -trained workers to southern provinces in recent years is an ongoing concern in the Northwest Territories. Government officials say that part of the solution to inducing people to stay—and encouraging them to come—is providing top-notch education, health care, and housing.

Recognizing that education is such a crucial factor in employment, the territory is seeking to lower teacher-to-student ratios and to foster programs that move school graduates into the workforce. Lawmakers recently mandated that the student-to-teacher ratio must be 16.5 children to 1 teacher—an initiative that has resulted in millions of dollars in additional spending. Student support funding, the government money that most affects this ratio and helps put teachers in classrooms and gives students needed materials, has risen to 15 percent of the total school budget a year ahead of the territory's mandated schedule. In addition, the territory's Early Childhood Development Action Plan includes programs and funding for speech development, literacy improvement, screening tools for developmental delay tests, and public nutrition concerns.

Providing affordable housing in the territory is a growing problem. In aboriginal villages exempt from community taxes, there is no local power to help subsidize lower-cost housing. In expanding communities where mining enterprises are growing, population growth is outstripping the housing

■ A Housing Crisis in Yellowknife

In 1999, with the Giant Mine seemingly on the verge of shutting down, Yellowknife appeared to be winding up an era. Just three years later, housing costs are soaring, new homes are being snapped up as fast as they can be built, and new apartments are being built all over the city. Commercial building and high-density housing construction permits are up 500 percent from 2001.

The rising price of gold and the growing diamond trades have brought hundreds of new families to Yellowknife. As a result, the city's housing supply is severely strained. And the boom is likely to continue. The Canadian Mortgage and Housing Corporation estimates that Yellowknife will need one hundred new housing units each year for the next twelve years to accommodate the thousands of families expected to move in during that time.

The demands are challenging for Yellowknife. While the government will eventually gain tax revenues from new residents, it cannot do so until new homes are completed and new people are in place. Thus, tax revenues tend to be behind the trends somewhat, meaning that programs are not funded rapidly enough to accommodate the new people.

Even so, the city sees the growth as positive. New jobs have been created for construction workers, and revenues are likely to grow. Even better for the city, the trend is likely to continue.

supply, sending rental and housing prices higher. Many residents find that their ability to pay for housing is reduced year by year. Government and industry leaders are scrambling to solve the housing problem. The territorial government has signed an agreement with the federal government that will bring $7.5 million to help low-income families across the territory cope with rising rents. Meanwhile, private companies are building homes at a record pace—prices of existing homes have gotten so high that many see building a home as a viable alternative.

Providing adequate health care for all of its citizens is also a challenge in the Northwest Territories. The federal government supplies much of the money for the universal and comprehensive health care coverage that all territory residents, like all Canadians, receive. As is the case elsewhere in the country, however, health care costs in the territory are rising, and the territorial government must find ways to stretch limited health care funds. Further, access to health services is a constant challenge in many northern communities, especially where roads are lacking. Hiring and retaining good doctors, nurses, and care attendants is particularly difficult. The health challenges in small communities can be overwhelming to a small, often underpaid staff. Workers are in demand nearly all hours of the day, and continual problems and isolation breed discouragement among workers.

The territory has developed a number of new initiatives to deal with such problems, including new investments in on-call centers to support front-line staff and projects to expand screening and treatment for tuberculosis and breast cancer. These initiatives reflect the territory's desire to cut health care costs over time by preventing major illnesses early on, while addressing the current soaring costs occurring across the country's health care system.

Building Tomorrow's Economy

While many social problems continue to persist in the North-west Territories, new economic developments provide a heady sense of promise. The territory is working rapidly to lure resource development companies, and the effort is paying off. Plans for a natural gas pipeline from the Mackenzie delta area are going forward after many years of debate and

■ *An aerial shot in the vicinity of Tulita shows the right-of way being cut for the planned natural gas pipeline down the Mackenzie River valley.*

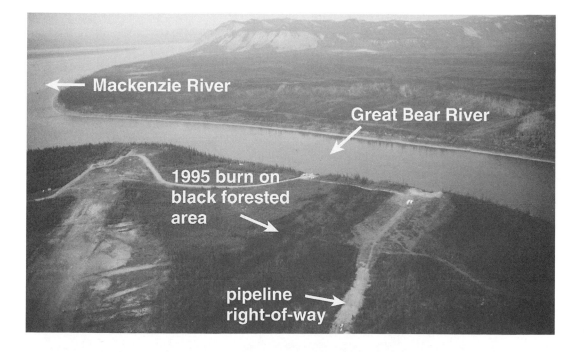

Mackenzie River

Great Bear River

1995 burn on black forested area

pipeline right-of-way

delay, and diamond mining is expanding. The territory is already a world-class producer of gem-quality stones, with new mines being developed that promise to boost the overall economy even more.

Business leaders in the Northwest Territories have been advocating the building of a natural gas pipeline from the Mackenzie delta area for decades. More than nine trillion cubic feet of gas are known to exist in the delta, with much more likely to be found. Natural gas companies believe that within a short time of operation, they could be moving nearly 800 million cubic feet of natural gas down the pipeline per day.

Today, government officials, a consortium of energy companies organized as the Mackenzie Delta Producers Group, and the native-owned Mackenzie Valley Aboriginal Pipeline Corporation have reached agreement on the most important issues. Most of the native land claims relating to the pipeline have been settled, guaranteeing aboriginal participation in the surveying, prospecting, and development of the pipeline. Resource-sharing agreements are also in place, meaning that aboriginals will not be left out of the profits coming from the pipeline. With research and development continuing, pipeline construction seems likely to begin by 2004, and it could be delivering natural gas to points south by 2008.

The Northwest Territories' government is now a strong supporter of the pipeline project and the Mackenzie Valley Aboriginal Pipeline Corporation. Government officials view the corporation as a potentially important new business model for native governments, according to the Department of Finance's 2002 Budget Address:

> [The Mackenzie Valley Aboriginal Pipeline Corporation] brings those with settled claims and economic resources together with those who are still striving towards these results. It is a worthy endeavour, whose success will mean prosperity not only for its shareholders, but for the entire Northwest Territories. For these reasons it merits government support and commitment. If the federal and territorial governments can share the vision, the vision can become reality. We will continue to provide support to the Mackenzie Valley Aboriginal Pipeline Corporation and accept a fair share of the financial risk if the Corporation is successful in securing federal government financial commitments to backstop its participation in the Mackenzie Valley Gas Pipeline.[21]

Nevertheless, many environmentalists continue to oppose the pipeline. They say that even low-impact drilling will upset

■ A Twenty-Five-Year Pipeline Delay

In the 1970s, federal officials and southern-based resource industry leaders looked to the Northwest Territories as a source of cheap energy in a time of inflation and soaring energy prices. Because seasonal sea ice in the Arctic Ocean limits shipping, a pipeline was proposed that would send natural gas from the Mackenzie delta down the Mackenzie River valley and into Alberta. From there existing transmission facilities could ship it throughout southern Canada. The plans generated a firestorm of controversy in the Northwest Territories, with environmentalists, native groups, government officials, and energy companies clashing over the proposed megaproject. In response, the federal government dispatched Thomas Berger, a British Columbia Supreme Court justice, to research the issue and make recommendations.

The inquiry Berger headed was unique in Canadian history. Berger traveled informally with his wife across the territory before the hearings even began, meeting with aboriginal leaders in their towns, hamlets, and homes. He held hearings in Yellowknife where he listened to some three hundred experts, and he held community hearings throughout the territory in town halls, community centers, even in tents and log cabins. Many of these hearings ended with traditional drum music, dancing, and food.

Berger encountered surprisingly strong feelings, as an incident at Fort Good Hope illustrates. Chief Frank T'Seleie, a young, university-educated tribal chief, confronted Robert Blair, president of Foothills Pipe Lines, with the following outburst: "You are the twentieth century General Custer. You are coming with your troops to slaughter us and steal land that is rightfully ours. You are coming to destroy a people that have a history of 30,000 years. Why? For twenty years of gas? Are you really that insane?"

The vehemence of such statements from aboriginals, environmentalists, and church leaders led Berger to recommend to the federal government in 1977 that a ten-year moratorium be placed on pipeline development until aboriginal land claims could be settled and environmental issues addressed. That process took longer than even Berger imagined.

many delicate habitats in the delta. Further, they say that a pipeline across the landscape will create a natural barrier that will interrupt many animals' migration patterns. Finally, environmentalists worry about the effects of environmental disasters, including explosions or leaks, that could wipe out populations of northern wildlife. Researchers say that they are investigating the best ways to make the drilling as environmentally friendly as possible, but critics believe that even small impacts could hurt sensitive areas.

A Boom in Diamond Mining

The other fastest growing sector of the Northwest Territories' economy is diamond mining. Diamond-related activities have boosted the population and economy in Yellowknife, and they could influence a much broader swath of the territory in the next ten years. The number of territorial companies servicing the diamond industry is growing, and territorial officials estimate that some 70 percent of the almost $1 billion spent on goods and services in the construction of the territory's first diamond mine, the Ekati diamond mine near Lac de Gras, northeast of Yellowknife, were purchased from northern businesses.

Diamond exploration began in the territory during the 1970s when prospectors found small concentrations of kimberlite, a type of rock that often contains significant numbers of the valuable gemstone. In 1991 geologists Charles Fipke and Stewart Blusson discovered diamonds at Point Lake in central Northwest Territories and set off the largest diamond-staking race in Canadian history. They are now co-owners (10 percent each) of the Ekati mine, along with BHP Billiton Diamonds. Ekati is a huge operation, involving six open pits, massive ore-extracting and -moving equipment, and a central

■ *These valuable rough diamonds have been cleaned and sorted but not yet cut into gems. Diamond mining is an important part of the Northwest Territories' economy.*

18,000-tons-per-day processing plant. Local environmental impacts are considerable, but the company says that "rehabilitation is an on-going, long-term aim."[22] The site is connected to Yellowknife by air and by a 310-mile (500-kilometer) seasonal ice road. Many employees are flown in from northern communities to work twelve-hour-per-day, two-week shifts and then flown home for two weeks off. The on-site residences are modern and comfortable, and workers also have access to extensive sports facilities and a 24/7 dining room offering free food.

The Northwest Territories' kimberlite deposits are now thought to be among the most extensive in the world. Within the past decade a score of diamond mine sites with strong potential have been identified, and hundreds of others are being explored. In order to gain regulatory approval from the territorial government, diamond producers have agreed to direct some of the diamonds to cutting and polishing plants within the territory. As a result, since 1999 three cutting and polishing plants have opened in the territory, all in Yellowknife, providing jobs for more than one hundred people and representing a growing chunk of the territory's manufacturing sector. Within several years, as more and more mines and diamond-servicing plants complete the regulatory review process, the Northwest Territories expects to become the diamond capital of North America, producing upwards of 12 to 15 percent by value of the world's gem-quality diamonds.

A Hopeful Future

The booming diamond industry and the renewed interest in a natural gas pipeline are the two most important recent developments in the Northwest Territories. How the residents and the government of the Territory handle these developments will go a long way in determining the territory's future. Along with the expected economic and employment benefits for years to come, resource extraction and industrial growth can be expected to strain the territory's limited services and present new challenges to its people, as its most recent budget summary acknowledged:

> The achievements that are bringing the benefits of economic growth are also producing pressures—pressures such as housing shortages, demands on community infrastructure and social and environmental concerns. We need to continue our efforts to promote economic growth and

prosperity but unless we do so in a manner that balances economic development and sustainable growth, we risk building our vision on an unstable foundation. This Budget is about maintaining that balance. We need to balance revenues with spending, to balance economic investments with social investments and to balance resource development with environmental protection.[23]

With the economy on the rise and the possibilities for sustainable growth expanding, the Northwest Territories sees much to be hopeful about. In addition to its apparently vast oil and natural gas resources, the territory can also boast considerable potential to develop more environmentally benign hydroelectric power. Its store of wilderness area is so vast that it could easily incorporate the fifth national park in the territory, on the east arm of Great Slave Lake, recently proposed by the federal government. As its year-round highway system expands and bridges begin to span major rivers, its potential for tourism could dwarf the forty thousand visitors who came in 2001 (and who spent some $40 million).

While social and cultural problems need to be addressed, residents believe that they are on the cusp of handling their own problems and solving some of their biggest challenges. Many difficulties remain before such challenges are met, but the hardy people of the north look to the future with hope.

Facts About the Northwest Territories

Government

- Form: Parliamentary system with federal and territorial levels
- Highest official: Premier, who administers territorial legislation and regulations
- Capital: Yellowknife
- Entered confederation: June 23, 1870 (first territory)
- Provincial flag: The territorial shield on a white center section, symbolizing ice and snow, between two blue sections, representing lakes and waters

Land

- Area: 452,478 square miles (1,171,918 square kilometers); 11.8% of total land of Canada; third-largest of provinces and territories; rivers and lakes cover 13.5% of Northwest Territories' land
- Boundaries: Bounded on the north by Beaufort Sea and Arctic Ocean, on the west by Yukon Territory, on the south by British Columbia, Alberta, and Saskatchewan, and on the east by Nunavut
- National parks: Aulavik, Nahanni, Tuktut Nogait, Wood Buffalo (mostly in Alberta)

- Territorial parks: twenty-seven, plus more than twenty recreation sites, regional parks, wildlife reserves
- Highest point: "Mount Nirvana," 9,098 feet (2,773 meters)
- Largest lake: Great Bear, 12,096 square miles (31,328 square kilometers), largest lake entirely within Canada and eighth-largest lake in world; Great Slave, 11,030 square miles (28,568 square kilometers), second-largest lake entirely within Canada and tenth-largest in world
- Other major lakes: Trout, Coleville, Lac La Martre, Keller, Fish
- Longest river: Mackenzie, 2,635 miles (4,241 kilometers) including tributaries; longest river in Canada and second-longest in North America
- Other major rivers: Great Bear, Liard, Slave, South Nahanni
- Time zones: Mountain Standard Time
- Geographical extremes: 60°N to approximately 78°N latitude; approximately 102°W to approximately 136°W longitude

Climate

- Greatest number of consecutive days with highest temperature above 90° F (32° C): 5, Hay River, July 26–31, 1984
- Coldest recorded windchill: −143° F (−97° C), Pelly Bay, January 13, 1975 (Canadian record)
- Average number of hours of sunshine during the summer: 1,037 (Canadian record)

People

- Population: 37,360 (2001 census); third-lowest population of provinces and territories; 0.1% of Canada's total population of 30,007,094
- Annual growth rate: −5.8% from 1996 to 2001 (third-slowest growth rate among provinces and territories; excludes loss of Nunavut in 1999)
- Density: 0.1 persons per square mile, compared to Canadian national average of 7.8 (0.03 and 3.0 persons per square kilometer)
- Location: 51% urban; 49% rural; 44% of residents live in the Yellowknife metropolitan area

- Predominant heritages: Aboriginal, British, French
- Largest ethnic groups: 50% of the population is aboriginal, including primarily Dene, Inuit, and Métis
- Major religious groups: Aboriginal religions, Catholic, Anglican
- Primary languages (first learned and still understood): 76% English, 22% aboriginal, led by Slavey, Dogrib, and Inuit, and 2% French
- Largest metropolitan areas: Yellowknife, population 16,541, a decrease of 4.2% between 1996 and 2001
- Other cities: none; largest towns: Hay River, Inuvik, Fort Smith
- Life expectancy at birth, 3-year average 1995–1997: Men 74.4 years; women 79.1; total both sexes 76.6; eleventh among provinces and territories (Canadian average: men 75.4; women 81.2; total 78.4)
- Immigration 7/1/2000–6/30/2001: 69, 0.03% of Canadian total of 252,088; third-lowest of provinces and territories
- Births 7/1/2000–6/30/2001: 679
- Deaths 7/1/2000–6/30/2001: 156
- Marriages in 1998: 142
- Divorces in 1998: 93

Plants and Animals

- Territorial bird: Gyrfalcon
- Territorial flower: Mountain aven
- Territorial tree: Tamarack
- Territorial fish: Arctic grayling
- Endangered, threatened, or vulnerable species: twenty, including Peary caribou, wood buffalo, grizzly bear, polar bear, wolverine, whooping crane, tundra peregrine falcon, short-eared owl, bowhead whale, and fourhorn sculpin

Holidays

- National: January 1 (New Year's Day); Good Friday; Easter; Easter Monday; July 1 or, if this date falls on a Sunday, July 2 (Canada's birthday); 1st Monday of September (Labour Day); 2nd Monday of October

(Thanksgiving); November 11 (Remembrance Day); December 25 (Christmas); December 26 (Boxing Day)

- Provincial: 1st Monday in August (civic holiday)

Economy

- Gross domestic product per capita: $44,980 in 1999, highest among provinces and territories and 132.9% compared to U.S. average[24]

- Gross territorial product: $2.2 billion at market prices in 2000, eleventh among the provinces and territories and 0.2% of gross national product

- Major exports: Oil, natural gas, diamonds, gold, fur

- Agriculture: Potatoes, hay, berries such as strawberries, raspberries, blueberries, and saskatoons, nursery and greenhouse products, livestock including deer, elk, bison

- Tourism: Hiking, sport fishing, hunting, adventure tourism, arts and crafts

- Main industries: Construction, transportation, warehousing, food and clothing products, printing

- Mining: Diamonds, gold, silver, tungsten, lead-zinc

Notes

Chapter 1: Land of the Northern Lights

1. Quoted in William L. Allen, ed., "Yukon and Northwest Territories" (map). Washington, D.C.: National Geographic Society, 1997.

2. Samuel Hearne, "Great Slave Lake," *Arctic Dawn: The Journeys of Samuel Hearne.* http://web.idirect.com.

3. Hearne, "Great Slave Lake."

4. J. David Henry and Michelle Mico, "The Birds of Aulavik National Park," *Taiga Net.* www.taiga.net.

5. James Conway, "The High Arctic," in *Canada's Wilderness Lands*, Donald J. Crump, ed. Washington, D.C.: National Geographic Society, 1982, p. 124.

Chapter 2: The First Peoples and European Exploration

6. Raymond de Coccola and Paul King, *The Incredible Eskimo: Life Among the Barren Land Eskimo*. Surrey, B.C.: Hancocke House, 1986, p. 16.

7. Hearne, "Great Slave Lake."

8. Quoted in Barry Gough, *First Across the Continent: Sir Alexander Mackenzie.* Norman, OK: University of Oklahoma Press, 1997, p. 79.

9. Quoted in David Morrison, "The Inuvialuit of the Western Arctic: From Ancient Times to 1902," First Peoples, *Civilization.ca.* www.civilization.ca.

Chapter 3: Toward the Twentieth Century

10. Roderick MacFarlane, "Letter from Roderick MacFarlane, Chief Factor, Fort Chipewyan, to David Laird, Lieut.

Governor of the North-West Territories, 24 December 1880," *National Archives of Canada*. www.archives.ca.

11. Ryan Silke, "A Detailed History of Tundra up to 1964," *Tundra Mine Heritage Project*. www.geocities.com.

12. *The People's Paths*, Paths to North American Indian Treaties, "Backgrounder Historic Indian Treaties, Indian and Northern Affairs Canada." www.thePeoplesPaths.net.

Chapter 4: Life in the Northwest Territories Today

13. *Canada 2000–2001*. Montreal: Ulysses Travel Guides, 2000, p. 659.

14. Quoted in Jonathon Gatehouse, "'It Belongs to Us': NWT's Premier Stephen Kakfwi on Resources, Pipelines and Sharing," *Macleans*, October 21, 2002. www.macleans.ca.

15. *Legislative Assembly of the Northwest Territories*, "Consensus Government." www.assembly.gov.nt.ca.

16. Terry Halifax, "Can the Consensus," *Inuvik Drum*, November 6, 2002. www.nnsl.com.

Chapter 5: Arts and Culture

17. Wayne Curtis et al., *Frommer's Canada*. New York: Macmillan, 1998, p. 779.

Chapter 6: A Territory in Transition

18. Thorunn Howatt, "Population Numbers Equal Cash," *Northern News Service*. www.nnsl.com.

19. Quoted in Gatehouse, "'It Belongs to Us.'"

20. Quoted in Gatehouse, "'It Belongs to Us.'"

21. *Government of the Northwest Territories Department of Finance*, "2002 Budget Address." www.fin.gov.nt.ca.

22. *Mining Technology*, Industry Projects, "Ekati Diamond Mine, Canada." www.mining-technology.com.

23. "2002 Budget Address." www.fin.gov.nt.ca.

Facts About the Northwest Territories

24. *Demographia*, "Canada: Regional Gross Domestic Product Data: 1999." www.demographia.com.

Chronology

ca. 3000 B.C. Ancestors of the Inuit arrive in the Arctic.

1576 British explorer Martin Frobisher makes his first expedition to the Arctic.

1670 Hudson's Bay Company is formed and given the rights to Rupert's Land.

1770 Samuel Hearne sets out to get to the Coppermine River.

1789 Alexander Mackenzie explores the great river route from Great Slave Lake to the Beaufort Sea.

1821 The Hudson's Bay Company merges with the North West Company.

1845 Arctic explorer John Franklin and 129 men sail for the Northwest Passage from England aboard two ships; the expedition gets stuck in ice near King William Island, and the entire crew perishes.

1870 The Canadian government purchases Rupert's Land from the Hudson's Bay Company and officially creates the North-West Territories.

1880 The arctic islands, previously under British jurisdiction, become Canadian, increasing the size of the North-West Territories.

1881 Manitoba is expanded by taking a chunk of land from the North-West Territories.

1882 Ontario is expanded by taking land from the North-West Territories.

1898   Quebec is expanded by taking land from the North-West Territories.

1899   The federal government creates the Yukon Territory from western North-West Territories, to better control the Klondike Gold Rush.

1905   Alberta and Saskatchewan provinces are formed from the southern portion of the renamed Northwest Territories.

1912   Borders for Manitoba, Ontario, and Quebec are adjusted northward; the Northwest Territories is now "Canada north of the sixty."

1930   Prospector Gilbert Labine spots a deposit of pitchblende on the eastern shores of Great Bear Lake, setting the stage for the Northwest Territories to become a major producer of radium.

1934   Geologists identify a seam of gold in Yellowknife Bay, touching off a gold rush and making Yellowknife a boomtown.

1940s   Construction of the Canol pipeline during World War II brings many nonnatives to the Northwest Territories.

1967   Yellowknife is chosen as the capital of the Northwest Territories.

1970   Dene Nation is incorporated.

1984   The Inuvialuit sign a land-claims agreement with the federal government.

1991   The discovery of diamonds at Point Lake in central Northwest Territories sets off the largest diamond-staking race in Canadian history.

1992   Nine gold mine workers are killed in an explosion in Yellowknife's Giant Mine during a labor conflict.

1999   Nunavut is formed from the eastern Northwest Territories.

2000   Dene leader Stephen Kakfwi is elected premier of Northwest Territories.

For Further Reading

Books

Scott Cookman, *Ice Blink: The Tragic Fate of Sir John Franklin's Polar Expedition*. New York: John Wiley, 2000. An exploration of the disastrous Franklin expedition with new theories about who might have been responsible for the tragedy.

Don Gillmor, Achille Michaud, and Pierre Turgeon, *Canada: A People's History*. Toronto: McClelland & Stewart, 2001. This two-volume reference book traces the development of Canada from its earliest settlement to modern times.

Roger E. Riendeau, *A Brief History of Canada*. Markham, Ontario: Fitzhenry and Whiteside, 2000. This readable survey of Canadian history includes many maps and illustrations.

Websites

The Canadian Encyclopedia (www.thecanadianencyclopedia. com). The web version of the three-volume printed work is authoritative and accessible.

The Government of the Northwest Territories (www.gov.nt.ca). The government's comprehensive website, including programs, park listings, recreational ideas, business information, and other data unique to the territory.

National Archives of Canada (www.archives.ca). An excellent place to find primary documents that shaped the development of Canada.

Statistics Canada (www.statcan.ca). A reliable source for thousands of statistics related to all aspects of Canadian life.

Works Consulted

Books

Canada 2000–2001. Montreal: Ulysses Travel Guides, 2000. The section on the Northwest Territories covers geography, history, and politics as well as accommodations, restaurants, and activities.

Raymond de Coccola and Paul King, *The Incredible Eskimo: Life Among the Barren Land Eskimo.* Surrey, B.C.: Hancocke House, 1986. Observations on the traditional life of an Inuit society.

Donald J. Crump, ed., *Canada's Wilderness Lands.* Washington, D.C.: National Geographic Society, 1982. A lavishly illustrated look at the country's many frontiers.

Wayne Curtis et al., *Frommer's Canada.* New York: Macmillan, 1998. A detailed travel guide.

Barry Gough, *First Across the Continent: Sir Alexander Mackenzie.* Norman, OK: University of Oklahoma Press, 1997. An exploration of Mackenzie's motivation as he dealt with native peoples and fellow traders in his relentless travels across the Canadian North.

Andrew Hempstead, *Alberta and the Northwest Territories Handbook.* Chico, CA: Moon Publications, 1999. Full of maps, photos, and illustrations, this book covers most of the natural wonders of the Canadian northwest.

Robert Glenn Ketchum, *Northwest Passage.* New York: Aperture, 1996. An inspiring photo account of a 1994 single-season east-to-west traverse.

J.H. Paterson, North America: *A Geography of the United States and Canada.* New York: Oxford University Press, 1994. A thoroughly researched discussion of Canadian and U.S. geography that helps explain the direct role of geography in regional economies.

Periodicals

William L. Allen, ed., "Yukon and Northwest Territories" (map). Washington, D.C.: National Geographic Society, 1997.

Graham Ashford and Jennifer Castelden, "Inuit Observations on Climate Change Final Report," Winnipeg, Manitoba: International Institute for Sustainable Development, 2001.

Douglas H. Chadwick, "Nahanni: Canada's Wilderness Park," *National Geographic*, September 1981.

"Northwest Territories 2001 . . . By the Numbers," Yellowknife: Bureau of Statistics, Government of the Northwest Territories, June 2001.

William C. Wonders, "Native Claims and Place Names in Canada's Western Arctic," *Canadian Journal of Native Studies,* vol. VII, no. 1, 1987.

Internet Sources

Demographia, "Canada: Regional Gross Domestic Product Data: 1999." www.demographia.com.

Jack Harley, "The Mad Trapper of Rat River," *Mysteries of Canada.* www.mysteriesofcanada.com.

J. David Henry and Michelle Mico, Reports, "The Birds of Aulavik National Park," *Taiga Net.* www.taiga.net.

Mining Technology, Industry Projects, "Ekati Diamond Mine, Canada." www.mining-technology.com.

David Morrison, First Peoples, "The Inuvialuit of the Western Arctic: From Ancient Times to 1902," *Civilization.ca.* www.civilization.ca.

Martin O'Malley, "The Mackenzie Valley Pipeline," *CBC News Online,* May 9, 2002. http://cbc.ca.

The People's Paths, Paths to North American Indian Treaties, "Backgrounder Historic Indian Treaties, Indian and Northern Affairs Canada." www.the PeoplesPaths.net.

Ryan Silke, "A Detailed History of Tundra up to 1964," *Tundra Mine Heritage Project*. www.geocities.com.

Websites

Arctic Dawn: The Journeys of Samuel Hearne (http://web.idirect.com). This online version of Hearne's diary makes fascinating reading for those interested in the Northwest Territories' first European explorer.

Canada's Digital Collections (http://collections.ic.gc.ca). Lists more than 400 websites detailing Canada's history, science, and technology.

Maclean's (www.macleans.ca). The online version of the popular Canadian weekly magazine has excellent archives and keeps abreast of new developments across Canada.

Northern News Service (www.nnsl.com). Yellowknife-based daily news, features, weather, market data, and more.

Index

Alaska Highway, 62
Amundsen, Roald, 35
Arctic Circle, 11
    exploration above, 34
    frost-free period above,
        12–13
    rain and snow below, 13
Aulavik National Park, 23
Aurora College, 67–68
Aurora Research Institute, 68

Banks Island, 22
Banks Island Bird Sanctuary
    No. 1, 23
Banks Island Bird Sanctuary
    No. 2, 23
Berger, Thomas, 91
BHP Billiton Diamonds, 61, 93
birds, 16, 20, 21, 23
Blackstone Territorial Park, 80
Blair, Robert, 91
Blusson, Stewart, 93
Button, Thomas, 30

Canada
    becomes dominion, 38
    early challenges to, 41–42
Canada-NWT Cooperation
    Agreement on Languages, 60
Canadian Mortgage and
    Housing Corporation, 89
Canadian Permanent Com-
    mittee on Geographical
    Names, 83
Canadian Shield, 13, 15
Canol (Canadian oil) Heritage
    Trail, 62

Canol pipeline, 62–63
Catholic School District (Yel-
    lowknife), 67
Chadwick, Douglas, 79
Charles II (king of England),
    38
Christian missionaries, 43–44,
    73
climate, 11–13
    harshness of, 7, 12–13, 64
    visual distortions caused by,
        16
Conflict of Interest Commis-
    sioner, 59
Con Mine, 50–51
Consolidated Mining and
    Smelting Company of
    Canada (Cominco), 49–50
Conway, James, 23
Curie, Marie, 48
Curie, Pierre, 48
Curtiss, Glenn, 47

Davis, John, 30
De Coccola, Raymond, 26, 27
Deh Cho, 32, 83
    see also Mackenzie River
Deh Cho Air, 83
Deh Cho Drum (newspaper), 83
Deline, 52–53
    life in, 56
    name change from Fort
        Franklin to, 83
Dempster Highway, 77–78
Dene, 7–8, 17, 28–30, 33, 48–49
    conflicts between Inuit and,
        30

cultural offerings of, 75
diversity of, 28, 29–30
epidemics decimate, 37, 40
land claim disputes, 51–53
societies, 28–29
Department of Education,
    67
diamond industry, 81, 85
    booming, 94
    expansion of, 86, 89
    impact on economy of,
        92–93
Dickins, Clennell, 48
Dog Derby, 70–71

Early Childhood Development
    Action Plan, 87
economy, 61–63
    effect of downturn in gold
        mining on, 82
    fur-based, 34
    influence of diamond min-
        ing on, 92–93
    resource-driven, 9, 10
    strains on services caused by
        growth in, 94
education, 65–68
    as crucial factor in employ-
        ment, 87
    federal government pay-
        ments for, 84
    focus on science and tech-
        nology in, 66
    higher, 67–68
    religious, 67
    teacher shortages, 86
Ekati diamond mine, 93

Eldorado Mining & Refining, 48, 49, 51

Erebus (ship), 34

Europeans
arrival of earliest, 30
diseases brought by, 37, 40
disruption of native way of life by, 8–9
interaction between Inuit and, 37
negative impact of, 25, 37, 40
tensions between natives and, 9

Fipke, Charles, 93

First Nations, 7–8, 29, 42
residential schools scandal and, 44–45

fishing, 19, 20, 22, 62

Foothills Pipe Lines, 91

forests, 15–16, 18, 21

Fort Providence Combined Council Alliance, 65

Franklin, John, 33, 48, 56
final expedition of, 34–35

Frobisher, Martin, 30

fur trade, 44–45, 73
effect on native peoples of, 34–35, 37
forts, 32, 33, 36–37
violence connected to, 34, 36

Gatehouse, Jonathon, 52

Giant Mine, 50–51
labor conflict, 52

Gilday, Leela, 74

Gjoa (ship), 35

Great Bear Lake, 15, 19, 20, 49, 56
uranium ore from, 49

Great Slave Lake, 14, 15, 46
first European to reach, 31
size of, 20

Halifax, Terry, 59

Harley, Jack, 73

Hearne, Samuel, 31–32
cooperation with native peoples of, 32
journal entries of, 13, 14, 15

Helen Kalvak School, 66

Howatt, Thorunn, 82

Hudson, Henry, 30

Hudson's Bay Company, 31, 34, 37, 38, 42

ice roads, 62, 64
seasonal, to Yellowknife, 93

Indian Residential Schools Resolution Canada, 45

Indian Territories Act, 38

Inuit, 7, 15, 17, 21
arctic lifestyle of, 24, 26
changes for, 36–37
coastal, 26–28
conflicts between Dene and, 30
differences between coastal and inland, 27
epidemics decimate, 37, 40
land claims lead to creation of Nunavut, 54
missionaries and government among, 43–45
whale-hunting techniques of, 28

Inuvik, 21, 59–60
as cultural capital of the north, 75–77
ice road connections to, 64

James, Thomas, 30

Johnson, Albert, 72, 73

Kakfwi, Stephen
attempts to change federal revenue agreements, 85
comments on Alexander Mackenzie, 33

as premier of Northwest Territories, 57, 58, 82

Kelsey, Henry, 30

kimberlite, 93
see also diamond industry

Klondike gold rush, 46

Labine, Gilbert, 48, 49, 51

Languages Commissioner, 60

Laurence, George, 49

MacFarlane, Roderick, 42

Mackenzie, Alexander (explorer), 32–33

Mackenzie, Alexander (prime minister), 33

Mackenzie Delta Producers Group, 90

Mackenzie Mountains, 12, 17–19, 62

Mackenzie River, 19–22, 53
delta, 21–22, 54, 55
exploration of, 32–33
importance of to native peoples, 29–30
new bridge proposed for, 65
possible name change for, 83

Mackenzie Valley Aboriginal Pipeline Corporation, 90–92

Mad Trapper. *See* Johnson, Albert

Manhattan Project, 49

McLeod, Frank, 79

McLeod, Willie, 79

Métis, 56, 83

mining, 20
diamond, 81, 85, 86, 89, 92–93
friction caused by, 51–53
gold, 46–47, 48, 49–51, 82
health problems associated with, 52–53
population growth connected to, 87
uranium, 49

mirages, 16

Miramar Mining Corporation, 51, 61

"Mysteries of Canada" (Harley), 73

Nahanni National Park, 79

National Research Council of Canada, 49

native peoples, 21–22

see also specific peoples

complex societies of, 25

early history, 7–18

effect of fur trade on, 34–35, 37

severe effects of European diseases on, 25, 37, 40

signing of treaties by, 42–43

see also treaties

tensions between newcomers and, 9, 54

underrepresentation of, in Nunavut government, 82

unemployment rate among, 86

natural gas pipeline project, 89–92

aboriginal participation in, 90

environmental concerns regarding, 92

opposition to, 91

supporters of, 90–91

twenty-five-year delay in, 91

natural resources, 10, 22, 41, 48, 53, 61, 94

federal government control over, 84–85

Norman Wells, fossil hunt in, 76

northern lights (aurora borealis), 7, 18, 61, 78

North West Company, 32, 34, 36

Northwest Passage

search for, 8, 25, 30, 31, 34–35

successful navigation of, 35

North-West Territories. *See* Northwest Territories

Northwest Territories

arctic islands, 22–24, 39, 45

arrival of airplanes and miners in, 47–48

artists, 76

arts and culture, 69, 71–72, 74–75

carving up of, 9, 46

challenges of, 7, 55, 61, 88–89

creating economic diversity in, 61–63

cultural diversity in, 60

diverse landforms of, 24

early government of, 42–43

employment, 61–63, 86, 87

evolution of, 38–39

exaggerated length of nights and days in, 7, 14

exciting prospects for, 81, 82, 94

festivals, 69–70, 72–73, 76

geography, 7, 9, 11, 22–23

geology, 13, 15, 24

government by consensus, 57–59

health care in, 9, 61, 81, 84, 87, 88–89

high cost of living in, 63–65, 84

housing problem in, 87–88, 89

influx of newcomers to, 46–48

isolation of, 7, 13, 55, 60–61, 88

landscape, 7, 11

languages, 59–61

Legislative Assembly, 57, 58, 59, 83

monetary relationship between federal government and, 84–85

multiculturalism, 10, 60

population, 9, 13, 47, 55–57

potential of economic self-sufficiency for, 85

present configuration of, 39

problems posed by creation of Nunavut and, 81–82

tax cuts in, 86

tourism, 7, 18, 20, 61, 62–63, 77, 94

transition from European to native names in, 83

see also climate; economy

Nunavut, 22, 44, 47

creation of, 9, 39, 54

early exploration of, 31

political tension in, 82

problems in Northwest Territories posed by, 81–82

Official Languages Act, 60

permafrost, 15–16

in tundra, 16

pingos, 21

plant life, 11, 14, 16, 17, 18, 21, 22

unusual, in Mackenzie Mountains hot springs areas, 19

Pond, Peter, 32

Prince of Wales Northern Heritage Centre, 36, 72

Rae, John, 34

Range Lake North elementary (K–8) school, 66

Richardson, John, 56

Royal Canadian Mounted Police, 44–45, 52, 72, 73

Royal Oak Mines, 52

Rupert's Land, 34, 38

sea ice, 11–12, 24

shipping limitations due to seasonal, 91

Silke, Ryan, 50

Smyth, D. McCormack, 49
Steinbruck, Jean, journal of, 36
Stuart, William, 30–31
sun globes ("sundaes"), 16

Tatti, Fibbie, 60
Terror (ship), 34
Thanadelthur, 31
treaties, 40, 42–43, 53
    problems arising from, 43,
        45
tree line, 15
T'Seleie, Frank, 91
Tuktut Nogait National Park,
    15
tundra, 15, 16–17, 22, 23
Twin Falls Territorial Park, 80

Victoria Island, 22, 31

"Waterfalls Route" (Highway
    1), 78, 80
whales, 21, 24, 28
    decimation of, 37
wildlife, 11, 15, 17, 18–19, 20,
    21, 22–24
    depletion of, 35, 37
    reliance of native peoples
        on, 29–30
Wonders, William C., 83
Wood Buffalo National Park,
    19
World War II, 49
    oil pipeline of, 62–63

XY Company, 36

Yellowknife, 20, 36, 47
    aftereffects of labor violence
        in, 52

art and theater in, 71–72
becomes capital of North-
    west Territories, 51
as cultural crossroads,
    69–71
education, 66–67
growth of, 50
housing crisis in, 89
importance of diamond-
    related activities to, 92–93
job growth in, 86, 89
mining in, 49–51
origin of name, 48–49
population, 55
seasonal ice roads to, 93
viewing northern lights
    from, 18
weather, 13
Yellowknife Administration
    District, 50

Picture Credits

Cover: © The Image Bank/Getty Images
© Aurora Research Institute, 67
© J.F. Bergeron, Parks and Tourism, Government of the NWT, 44, 78
© James Bird/NWT Archives, 47, 50
© M. Burgess, Geological Survey of Canada, Natural Resources Canada, 89
© Canada Tourism Commision, 15, 79
© Canadian Heritage Gallery, NWT Economic Development and Tourism, 17
© Canadian Heritage Gallery, National Archives of Canada, 18, 26, 29, 31
© Canadian Heritage Gallery, after T. Lawrence, National Archives of Canada, 33
© Diavik Diamond, Inc., 92
© Leela Gilday, 74
© Fran Hurcomb, Parks and Tourism, Government of the NWT, 70, 71, 75,
© Michelle Krouse, 66
© Legislative Assembly of the NWT, 58, 59
© Tessa Macintosh, Parks and Tourism, Government of the NWT, 9, 20, 84
© National Archives of Canada, 29, 31, 33
© Ben Nind, 72
© Northwest Territories Department of Information/NWT Archives, 51
© Parks and Tourism, Government of the NWT, 14
© Wolfgang Weber, Parks and Tourism, Government of the NWT, 24, 63
© Douglas Wilkinson/NWT Archives, 21, 28
© Michael S. Yamashita/Corbis, 85

About the Authors

Gordon D. Laws graduated with a Bachelor of Arts in English from Brigham Young University. He is the author of several short stories, numerous magazine articles, and the novel *My People*. Currently, he is a freelance writer and editor. Lauren M. Laws graduated with a Bachelor of Arts in history from Brigham Young University. She is a researcher and records expert. In addition to this work, Gordon and Lauren collaborated on *Exploring Canada: Alberta* and *Exploring Canada: Manitoba*. Gordon and Lauren live in Massachusetts with their son, Grant.